DISCIPLINES
of Holy Living

DISCIPLINES
OF *Holy* LIVING

BY KEITH DRURY

WESLEY PRESS
P.O. Box 50434
Indianapolis, Indiana 46250

DISCIPLINES OF HOLY LIVING
Copyright (©) 1989 by Keith Drury

Wesley Press
P.O. Box 50434
Indianapolis, Indiana 46250-0434

Library of Congress Cataloging in Publication Data

Drury, Keith W.
   Disciplines of Holy Living
   Wesley Press: Indianapolis, Ind.: Keith Drury ©1989.
   1. Holiness. 2. Sanctification. I. Title
        ISBN 0-89827-069-3

All Scripture passages, unless otherwise indicated, are from the New International Version © 1987 by New York International Bible Society.

All rights reserved. No part of this publication may be reproduced, stored in a retrieval system, or transmitted in any form or by any means – electronic, mechanical, photocopy, recording, or any other – except for brief quotations in printed reviews, without the prior permission of the publisher.

Printed in the United States of America

Dedicated to:
the memory of my brother,
Elmer Drury

Contents

Preface 9

1. How Christians Change: Crisis and Process . 11
2. Restitution: Making Things Right 31
3. Grudges: Forgiving Old Hurts 47
4. Thought Life: Overcoming Impure Thoughts 59
5. Restoration: Restoring a Fallen Christian . 75
6. Humility: Putting Off Pride 91
7. Ambitions: Abandoning Selfish Ambition . 109
8. Honesty: Speaking Absolute Truth 127
9. Peacemaking: Mending Broken Relationships . 143
10. What to do When Your Light is Brighter Than Your Life 161

Preface

Disciplines of Holy Living? What are they? What does this word "Discipline" suggest to you? Does it remind you of serious daily devotions? Extended times of fasting? Fervent periods of prayer?

Granted, these acts of personal piety are related to holy living. But this book is about the lesser known disciplines of holiness. Some chapters are about *inner personal* disciplines of obedience . . . releasing grudges, overcoming impure thoughts, putting off pride, and abandoning selfish ambition. Other chapters address *interpersonal* disciplines . . . making restitution, restoring a fallen Christian, speaking with truthfulness, and mending broken relationships. These lesser known disciplines of holy living are desperately needed in today's church.

The gospel is such a positive message of hope! Not just for unbelievers, but for Christians too. The message of Christ marches into our pessimistic world declaring "you can change!" You really can! God's great plan of salvation extends beyond establishing our holiness in *position* – perfect in Christ Jesus. It provides for the actual transformation of our daily *performance* into Christlikeness.

You can obey Him! You can "walk as Jesus walked" (1 John 2:6). Not only in the areas this book deals with, but in dozens . . . no, hundreds, of other areas. Holiness is *obedience.* It is following Jesus, step by step, walking in submission to Him. Why? Because we love Him.

And this is love: that we walk in obedience to his commands.
— 2 John 6

1

HOW Christians Change

Crisis and Process

If we walk in the light, as he is in the light, we have fellowship with one another, and the blood of Jesus, his Son, purifies us from all sin.

—1 John 1:7

This book is about change. It will be hard to read it without becoming different. This book is about becoming more than you are. Each chapter deals with specific areas where God might be nudging you to change. They are disciplines of obedient living.

Yet before we deal with these individual disciplines of holy living, we should consider a more basic question — How do Christians change? God has a plan for changing Christians like you and me from what we used to be, into what we've become, and finally into everything we could be. Understanding how God's changing power works may help us in dealing with the individual chapters.

Salvation – an outside job

Salvation is both an inside and an outside job. Many of the changes at your conversion were outside changes. For instance, the moment you accepted Christ into your life you were "justified." In justification God decreed that you were no longer liable for your sins – it was "just-as-if-I'd" never sinned. This didn't happen in your heart, it happened outside of you at God's throne in heaven. And you were "pardoned." A pardon doesn't occur *in* a person; it happens outside of a person. It is a change of status. Pardoning pictures a legal transaction in the courts of heaven. When you came to Christ you were also "adopted" into the family of God . . . you became God's son or daughter. Here is another legal term, something happening outside you changing your status. When you started this walk with Christ lots happened outside of you. Your status was changed, your position was new.

Salvation – an inside job

But God didn't limit His "great plan of salvation" to outside transactions. He works within too. When you received Christ you were "born again" or "regenerated." You became a new person inside; the old life passed away and you were reborn inside . . . things became new. And when you received Christ you were "made alive in Christ," experiencing your own personal resurrection. Before you were saved, you were, for all spiritual purposes, "dead in trespasses and sins." Then through faith you became "alive unto Christ." None of these things happened outside of you – they were all "inside jobs."

Conversion – a changing event

Becoming a Christian is a life-changing event. In a single moment you were brought to life inside. In an instant God changed areas of your life. In the weeks following your conversion you may remember noticing new desires, different values, and fresh interests. God had changed you inside. Perhaps you immediately dropped some habit. Others may have noticed a change in you. Someone may have said, "You seem different." The experience is almost universal – people change at the crisis of conversion. In a moment God changes you in some areas.

But you weren't changed enough!

But sooner or later every new Christian recognizes that *many things didn't change.* Your position may have been "perfect in Christ" but your performance was obviously less than perfect. Then you became painfully aware of attitudes, thoughts, words, and actions which were out of character with who you really were. This is a serious predicament for the new Christian. The euphoria of conversion is gone. The dramatic inner changes of those first few weeks and months has dimmed. Now you forget how much change has already happened. You begin to look at all the change that hasn't happened. This is a serious juncture and several routes are possible at this crossroads:

(1) Give up. Some new Christians simply quit the race at this point. Consider this letter:
"I was so excited last summer when I got saved. I thought it had solved all my problems. Was I ever wrong! Now the excitement has worn off and I'm a mess. There are so many areas of my life out of whack, I'm such a lousy Christian, I'm afraid I'll never get straightened out. I lose

my temper at work and say some things I know Christians shouldn't say. There is one particular sinful habit I've had for years that I just can't shake – I've tried over and over but I fail every time. My pastor says I should be witnessing, and I did when I was first saved, but now I'm afraid to. What has happened to me? I feel like a worse sinner than before I was saved. I feel like just giving up."

Giving up is really no solution at all. The Christian who gives up on changing, either drifts back into his or her old life, or settles into cool-hearted nominal Christianity. Giving up is not the answer.

(2) Refocus on position. Some advise the new Christian at this point to refocus their thoughts on their position in Christ, taking away their concern for personal sin. "Don't look at your sin . . . focus on your position as "perfect in Christ." "God can't see your sin – you are in Christ and God sees only the perfection of Christ – so don't waste time looking at your sin." "Your sin simply tells you the kind of person you really are . . . it shows how sinful humanity is, let your sin be a reminder for you to praise God for the perfect Christ." "Of course, you are still a sinner, but you are a saved one now. Remember, 'There is therefore no condemnation to those that are in Christ Jesus' . . . keep saying that verse and recognize that your sins are forgiven – past, present and future."

While this route offers some relief to the new Christian burdened by personal sin, it is not the ultimate answer. Anyone who reads the New Testament keeps discovering repeated calls to obedience. God continually calls His children to put off sin. Would God constantly call us to obedience if it were impossible? Would God tease us with a command which we could not obey? The new Christian often feels down deep inside that there is more to this Christian walk than focusing on position.

The new Christian's instincts are right – there must be a way to bring our performance up to our position. We needn't spend the rest of our lives dismissing our sin by refocusing our thoughts on our perfect position in Christ. God's plan of salvation is more complete than that.

This brings a third route into focus – the biblical solution: Become what you are!

3. Sanctification. It's a big word and often misunderstood. But it is a necessary word and work. *Sanctification is God's work inside us to transform us into Christlikeness.* It is everything God does in us to make us like His Son Jesus. It begins the moment we are saved . . . this is called "initial sanctification." At conversion God changes us in certain areas so that, in an instant, we become more like Jesus in this thought, or that desire, this attitude, or that word or action.

But God's sanctifying work doesn't end at conversion. "Initial sanctification" is just the beginning of a great journey with Christ . . . walking in the light, becoming more like Jesus week by week, year by year. It is a journey of hearing God speak, making commitments, allowing God to change, adjust, correct, transform, and mold us after His will. This continual work of inner change is called "Progressive Sanctification." It is God's way of making us more like Jesus.

If only new Christians could be told of this way out – a route to spiritual growth. Maybe then they would be less likely to give up on living the Christian life. Or maybe they would do more than dismiss their sinful performance by focusing on their position in Christ. If only more Christians could be told of God's full plan of salvation. He proposes to bring your imperfect performance up to your perfect position! God will bring the good work He began in us at conversion to completion (Phil. 1:6).

Position and Performance

These are the wonderful ways of God – He not only changes our *legal position* outside of us, but He intends to change our *daily performance* by changing us inside. In other words, God's plan of salvation is more than a simple outside change of status – (from "lost sinner" to "saved sinner"). He actually proposes to change our performance as well (from "saved sinner" to "obedient child") He intends to change us on the inside – eliminating selected thoughts, words and deeds, and adding new thoughts and attitudes, language patterns, and personal habits of action. This is God's plan to change your position and your performance.

If you have already received Christ, then there is nothing more you can do to change your position. You are already "risen with Christ," adopted, forgiven, pardoned, and justified. There is absolutely nothing you can do (or that God could do, for that matter) to improve your position with God. You are "sealed" and have received the Holy Spirit as God's down payment, guaranteeing what you will receive in the future. Your legal position is already "perfect in Christ." Your position can not be improved.

But performance is another matter altogether. Wouldn't you readily admit the need of growth in your day-to-day walk in obedience . . . your *performance?* Though nothing can be done to improve your outside standing with God, is there not much to be done to improve your inside obedience to Him?

God does inside jobs. He wants the freedom to work inside you to transform your values, attitudes, language, habits, thoughts – making them conform to those of Jesus Christ.

How does He do this? What is God's process of sanctification? How does He go about changing your thoughts, words, deeds, and attitudes? That is the subject of this chapter.

Big Event Changes

Conversion is a big event. In this momentous spiritual event, God performs major changes in us – we become "new creatures" in Christ as the old passes away. In a week or a month we notice dozens of changes God has concentrated into conversion, the major spiritual event of our lives. Conversion is a big event change in our life.

Being filled with the Spirit is a second crisis event. One moment you were not yet filled, and the next moment you become filled with the Spirit. The disciples were radically changed when they were filled with the Spirit (Acts 2). A fearful failing Peter became the bold preacher unafraid to lose his life for Christ. John, a "son of thunder" who was ready to destroy a whole Samaritan village with fire became the "apostle of love" (Luke 9:54). Fearful disciples who had cowered behind locked doors became bold soldiers of the cross who filled Jerusalem with their teaching.

When the Holy Spirit fills a man or a woman changes happen . . . instantly. This is a second "Big Event Change." These two experiences – conversion and the filling of the Spirit – are widely recognized as crisis change events in a Christian's life. In fact, some would attempt to squeeze *all* change into these two events. But there are many other changes which God performs in His sanctifying work – making us more like Christ – which do not occur during these two major events. These are the changes which happen progressively.

How Christians Change

Christians are supposed to change. God yearns to keep working on and in us, moving us toward perfection (2 Cor. 13:9). Though God works in mysterious ways, adapting His methods for each individual, there are some general patterns to His work at progressively sanctifying His children. Most Christians will recognize that God's changing process often occurs in these five stages:

1. Dawning Awareness Stage

God always moves first. We are never the initiators, we are always the responders. He took the first step in our salvation . . . sending His Son "while we were still sinners" (Romans 5:8). God is always reaching, calling, searching. So it is with our sanctification. God begins the changing process by making us aware of a need first. We begin to sense an area of our life is "out of sync" with God's will for us.

He does this through His Holy Spirit, God's invisible presence in us. God's Spirit "speaks" to us through our thoughts. He guides, corrects, convicts, and enlightens our mind to understand Bible truths. And He makes us *aware* of an area needing change.

This awareness often comes slowly . . . like the dawn. First there are tiny hints of gray, then gradually the light increases – from charcoal black, to dark gray, to light gray, to pale gray – then finally the sun bursts over the horizon filling the land with its beams of bright light.

So the Holy Spirit often makes us aware of areas needing change. We read an article, hear a testimony, or a certain Bible passage jumps out at us. This is new! Is this really God's way and will? Is this true? Is this for me? Is it possible? These are the questions that indicate God is making us aware of a new area where He intends to change us.

Often God is making us aware of many areas at once. As we associate with other Christians, read good Christian literature, and get into God's Word, we gradually become aware of areas where our lives fall short of God's perfect standard. We could list habits we need to stop, others we ought to start. We see places where we are less than we ought to be. This is the "Dawning Awareness" stage. It is the first step God takes in His process of changing us.

2. Growing Conviction Stage

Out of the areas we are aware of which need changing, God now begins to focus on one. He zeroes in on a particular attitude, or a certain habit, or one language pattern and keeps coming back to it. This is different than mere awareness – now we are becoming convinced we *must* change. The Holy Spirit gradually puts greater pressure on us . . . both logically and emotionally as He convinces us of our need for change. This is the "Growing Conviction" stage. The Holy Spirit is getting us ready for God's changing power in our lives.

One danger at this point is the Christian's feeling of condemnation. Sometimes a sensitive Christian has difficulty tuning in to the Holy Spirit's inner "still small voice." As they experience "Dawning Awareness" of dozens of areas in need of changing, they mistakenly assume God is convicting them of *all* these at once. Recognizing that change in so many areas at once seems unlikely, they become easy prey for Satan's condemnation. The Accuser loves few things better than to turn a Christian inward into defeat and despair by accusing him or her of being a miserable Christian. He is skillful at "quoting" the Bible to browbeat and intimidate sensitive saints.

God seldom convicts a Christian in many areas at once. The Holy Spirit's operations are done with a spiritual scalpel, not a butcher knife. How can you tell the difference between Satan's voice and the Holy Spirit's? Satan condemns, the Holy Spirit convicts. Satan's *condemnation* makes you feel like giving up, like you'll never make it, resulting in spiritual depression, discouragement, and a feeling of hopelessness. On the other hand, the Holy Spirit's *conviction* is accompanied by expectation and hope.

The Holy Spirit convinces men and women of sin, but never does so with a whip . . . it is with the positive hope of change. If Satan is discouraging you with the multiple areas where you are imperfect, turn your ear inward to the Holy Spirit's voice. He is probably aiming at one change target, trying to grant you the hope for change. The Spirit usually works with a narrowly aimed rifle shot of conviction, not a shotgun of condemnation.

There is a second danger at the "Growing Conviction" stage: trying to change yourself. It is at this stage when many Christians make repeated attempts to turn over a new leaf . . . trying to change in their own power. These attempts are common, but are destined to failure. You do not have the spiritual power to transform yourself into Christlikeness. This power is God's and God's alone. Any attempt to make yourself holy will produce only failure or a false righteousness leading to pride.

It took me far too long to discover this important truth about change. Numerous attempts at becoming holy in my own power were always accompanied with resounding failures. I discovered this truth and wrote in the front of my Bible, "When I try, I fail . . . When I trust . . . He succeeds." Trying to be holy will fail every time! Trusting Christ to make me holy will never fail!

This conviction is a growing one. Gradually the Spirit convinces us we must put off this, or put on that. Bible verses leap out at us, testimonies of other Christians who have been victorious in that area raise our hopes, magazine articles meet our eyes. We never realized there was so much said about this particular area! We are experiencing "Growing Conviction." God has gotten us ready for the third stage of change.

3. Crisis Decision Stage

So far in the growth process God took the lead.

He provided the dawning awareness of our needs, and He produced our growing conviction. Now God turns to us . . . it is our move.

Somewhere in the process of growing conviction we become convinced that we must change. At this point we recognize that to delay change any longer would be outright disobedience. Up until now God was patient with our slowness to realize our need, and even our sluggishness in sensing His conviction. But now we are convinced that THIS AREA MUST CHANGE. It is not our idea, but God's. We sense Him saying "It's your move now . . . are you with my program to change you, or not?"

Not that all this happens in a single moment in time. It may be a "stage" as the title suggests. God is not so autocratic that His invitations to grow come with sixty-second deadlines. The "Crisis Decision Stage" may occur over several days or even weeks. But when I am fully convinced that God is saying "I'm ready to change you" yet I drag my feet, refusing to be changed, I place myself in spiritual jeopardy. Once I am convinced that this is God speaking . . . and He is waiting for my reply, I'd better get with it, and cooperate with His program to change me. At some point resistance becomes rebellion. We cannot presume where that point will be . . . but there is a line of rebellion a foot-dragging Christian can cross.

So what is my move? *God calls me to make a decision to change – begin relying on God's power.* God is asking me to walk away from the action, habit, thought pattern or language by a crisis decision to change. But that decision is not a self-improvement action . . . the decision is one of trust, not trying. At this moment I abandon the sin He has been convicting me to put off, or I initiate the behavior or attitude He has called me to put on. My will is submitted, I have settled the question. By faith I accept God's changing power. I've settled the question – I *will* be changed, through Christ's power.

Now it's God's move again.

4. "Changing Grace" Stage

God is in the business of changing people. His "grace is sufficient" to meet all our changing needs. His power is mighty . . . like that which raised Jesus Christ from the dead . . . this is the power that works in us (Eph. 1:19-20). When Christians become convinced that God wants to change them, and they make a willful decision to trust His changing power, God acts. Most Christians could tell of several areas where they settled the issue at one point – perhaps at a retreat, in a church service, or at their bedside – and they were changed in an instant. The sinful thought, word or habit disappeared into thin air and they were never troubled by it again. This instantaneous transformation does occur. In a moment God sometimes completely transforms a particular area of your life.

But not always. Sometimes God's "Changing Grace" works gradually. Instead of a dramatic immediate transformation God *begins* a gradual changing process. When you "settled the question" things started to change, but you waited weeks, maybe months to experience complete wholeness in this area. Some changes of direction occur like tiny PT boats turning sharply in a moment, quickly heading in a new direction. Other changes happen like lumbering aircraft carriers . . . gradually bringing the ship about in a wide circle.

Why? Why doesn't God always change us instantaneously? Who knows? These are the ways of the Mighty One. Like physical healing, God sometimes grants complete wholeness in an instant . . . these we call miracles. But at other times God heals us over time . . . days and months, until finally we are back to full physical health. Likewise He heals spiritually . . . sometimes in a moment . . . we like it this way. But at other times He begins the changing process in response to our crisis decision. Either way, it is God who performs the changing.

One more little twist in the process ought to be mentioned. Sometimes there is a lag between stage three and four. For example, you have fully made your crisis decision and await God's changing grace . . . but it doesn't come. Upon reexamining your motives, you discover they are pure, and He has indeed convicted you of this change. You feel you have fully decided to change, you "received it by faith" and you trust in His power alone to change you. Yet you remain unchanged. What then? What should you do when it seems God is "stonewalling" you?

The answer is to wait. Wait on the Lord until He moves. Tarry. Don't run off in discouragement, tarry until He grants changing grace. Seek! Seek until you find the change you need. Hunger! Hunger and thirst for complete holiness in this area until you are satisfied. Get the idea? If you encounter a delayed response from God, hang in there . . . keep on seeking, and you will receive. Why does God do this? Why does He seem to withhold His changing grace at times? Who knows? These are the ways of the Mighty One. Your job is not to understand Him, it is to obey Him.

But, seek Him with all your heart. Be careful not to use the delay as an excuse to nurse thoughts, language, or actions which are improper for God's holy people. Don't take Satan's bait of suggesting that because God has delayed His cleansing or empowering that the presence of sin or the lack of power in your life is somehow God's fault. "I asked God to take it away but He didn't" is no excuse for more sin! Seeking is an intense, fervent activity. It is not a hangout for lazy Christians wanting to excuse sin for one more week or month. Seek Him pointedly, passionately, with a fervent spirit . . . then you will find the transforming power for which you hunger. Keep seeking, the change will come!

5. Disciplined Obedience

When the change occurs – whether instantaneously or gradual – the change is not complete. God does not make spiritual robots out of us. And He does not ban Satan from further temptations in that area. What He does is free us from the bondage of a specific thought or language pattern, habit, or activity. We are now free to choose God's way.

Perhaps you've heard someone tell of how God delivered them from the bondage of a certain sin. They closed their testimony off with something like ". . . and I never once since then have even had a desire to do it again." Perhaps you were discouraged. You wondered why God didn't do a complete job on you. Be careful. Who can figure the ways of the Mighty One? For some He works in an instant, for others gradually. Some He completely delivers from the desire to ever do it (or say or think it) again and temptation in this area loses its grip on them. These seem to need little "Disciplined Obedience" in this particular area. That stronghold of Satan seems to disappear. For most others it is not so. For this second group the magnetic backward pull remains and there now begins a step-by-step walk of "Disciplined Obedience."

This stage is cooperative . . . it is neither God's move nor yours anymore. Both of you move. You walk together as you discipline yourself to resist this old temptation. As you keep in step with God's light . . . neither turning left nor right off the road of obedience, the blood of His Son, Jesus keeps on cleansing you from all sin.

This is the walk of "Disciplined Obedience." You were convinced God wanted to change you and you made the crisis decision to trust His power to do it. He responded with changing grace and now you have new power to resist this old temptation. So you walk together, in harmony and experience the fellowship and joy of walking obediently in an area where you once thought you'd never find victory. Praise the Mighty One for His great plan of salvation – a scheme which not only changed our position before His throne . . . but goes beyond that to change our day-to-day performance as well. What a great idea!

What next?

This whole change process brings a deep-seated joy and fellowship with God. But what next? After a period of solidifying and assimilating your new growth, what does God do? He doubles back and points out another area of "Dawning Awareness" beginning to build a new area of conviction in your heart! And so goes the process, on and on. Constantly changing you into an image of His perfect Son Jesus Christ.

Now what about you, my friend?

Do you see where all this is headed? Do you see what God proposes to do? He intends to make you like Jesus Christ. If you'll let Him.

This book outlines various disciplines of holy living. Some chapters will make you aware of areas God will begin working on you about later. For now, these chapters will contribute one more ray of light as you approach the full dawning of God's leading in this area. You may not feel compelled to act on what you have read immediately. But likely somewhere else in this book lies a chapter just for you. Perhaps it deals with an area God has already been convicting you about. Reading the chapter will bring God's conviction to completeness . . . you'll be convinced that you *must* change. It will be time for a crisis decision.

I encourage you to open your heart to the Lord. He doesn't want to batter you with His truths. Rather, He wishes to lead you gently on to holiness and completeness if you will listen to His promptings and respond with commitment and trust. Try Him. You can trust Him.

Bible Study

1. Ephesians 2:1-2. In what ways was your life without Christ like being "dead"?

2. Romans 5:8. How did God demonstrate His great love for me even before I accepted Him?

3. 2 Corinthians 5:17. In what ways is the new Christian changed? In what ways is he or she often *not* changed?

4. Ephesians 2:6. Describe our position as a believer resulting from our salvation. What does this mean to you?

5. Ephesians 1:13-14. What way do we know that we really will receive all God has promised us?

6. 2 Corinthians 13:9. What was Paul's prayer for the Corinthian believers?

7. *Philippians 1:6.* What was the confidence Paul had for the Christians in the Philippian church?

8. *Hebrews 10:14.* How does this verse connect with the ideas of "position" and "performance"?

9. *1 John 3:1-3.*

   — What is our primary relationship to God?

   — What is the "hope" that we can have?

   — What should that hope prompt us to do?

10. *1 Peter 1:22.* The chapter said that any attempts at self-purification were doomed to failure. How does this Scripture explain how a Christian purifies himself?

11. *Philippians 3:16.* In what way does Paul use the idea of "position" and "performance" in this Scripture?

12. *1 Thessalonians 5:23-24.*

   — In this prayer for these Christians, what is Paul praying for?

— How extensive does he expect this sanctification to be?

— Who does it?

13. *Personal Reflection.*

— In what areas has the Lord been giving me dawning awareness, where I've come to sense that He will eventually do something in these areas?

— In what area or two might the Lord be giving me "Growing Conviction?" I'm not sure yet, but I think He might be zeroing in on these one or two areas:

— Is there an area where you believe God has already said "It's your move" and you need to make a "Crisis Decision" of obedience?

— Can you think of a time when you really did all you could and trusted God, yet you had to wait for His "Changing Grace"?

14. Final reflection. Is there something you could or should do in response to the truth you discovered in this chapter?

– An action to take?

– A promise to make?

2
RESTITUTION:
Making Things Right

> . . . I strive always to keep my conscience clear before God and man.
>
> Acts 24:16

always wanted to have a mustache. I heard somewhere in grade school that if you shaved your face, your beard would grow out dark and stubby. I think the argument was that a fellow ought to wait as long as possible before starting to shave. I took it quite the opposite. I gathered my dad's shaving mug, his chrome Gillette razor, locked myself in the bathroom and shaved off my imaginary beard. It didn't work. The fuzz merely regrew as fuzz.

Several years later when I was in seventh grade,

my church youth group had a Halloween party. I had no outfit for the party that night. My friend John and I stopped off at the local J. J. Newberry's store on the way home from school to shop. Among the array of Halloween masks and outfits was a first-rate stick-on mustache packaged in a nifty little plastic case. I could imagine myself with this mustache Friday night causing all the seventh grade girls to swoon. I tried it on. Somehow it made me feel taller, more manly, mature. The problem: I had no money.

I don't think I'd ever stolen anything before that. I slipped that little mustache in the right pocket of my school jacket and sneaked out to the street. I wore it to the party. The girls didn't swoon.

I had a hard time forgetting that mustache. I knew I was wrong, and that I should go back to the store, confess I had stolen the mustache, and pay for it. But I was afraid. I feared both the embarrassment and the penalty. A lady who worked at Newberry's attended the church where my dad pastored. I figured she'd tell him, and my dad would punish me like the thief I was. I conjured up all kinds of "worst case scenario" endings. I kept remembering the large flier posted near the entrance to that store. It had a drawing of a teenager peering through the bars in a jail cell. Above his sad face were the words "Shoplifters go to jail."

I could visualize a whole newspaper spread on how nice teens – even a preacher's son – could go bad. *I* would be the illustration. Parents would whisper after church, "Doesn't it make your heart ache . . . you know, how the Drury boy turned out!" They would admonish each other, "Keep a tight rein on your kids or they'll turn out like the *preacher's kid*."

So I never went back. Each time I recalled my offense, I'd try to ignore it, excuse it, or dismiss it. At first I told myself I couldn't afford making things right. I simply didn't have the money. The mustache had already lost its stickiness, so returning it wouldn't suffice. I didn't want to get my friend John in trouble either. I figured they'd send him up as an accessory or something. Mostly I just put it off. I intended to make it right . . . eventually.

With time my conviction gradually disappeared and I almost forgot about it. Occasionally guilt would surface but I would dismiss it with comments like, "It was such a little thing," or, "Oh my, that was a long time ago." I graduated from high school and moved away to college, forgetting the little mustache. For the most part, that is.

Except that every time I'd hear about "restitution" I'd remember the little mustache. When I'd read about restitution in an article, or hear someone share a testimony about a restitution they had made, that mustache would come slithering back to haunt me. The mustache was always there, reminding me of an unmade restitution.

At a retreat two decades later, God convinced me of the necessity of this restitution. It was clear I'd better fix it soon. I knew if I delayed much longer it would be more than foot dragging — it would be outright disobedience, even rebellion.

Within a month I was in the area with my family. I loaded my five-year-old boy into the car and went to make restitution for what I had stolen 20 years before. I explained to my son what I had done and what I was about to do. Frankly, all the way to the store I was secretly hoping it had gone out of business. It hadn't. David was intrigued by this whole idea. He seemed to get a kick out of seeing his dad be humbled.

After paying for the mustache, we returned to the car and headed out of town. My son had said nothing throughout the whole process. I could sense his mind whirling. As we drove up the entry ramp of the interstate, he turned and said, "You know, Dad, it would be better if you'd never take things . . . then you wouldn't have to go back like that."

I think he got the point. I know I got *David's*

point!

Restitution is going back and making things right for things you took or the people you hurt. It is "restoring" to the original owner what is rightfully theirs – property or respect and reputation. Restitution is returning a tool box taken from the company years ago. It is paying for a stack of office supplies you slipped out of the office without anyone's knowledge. It is paying taxes on unreported income you hid from the tax man. Restitution is large utility companies granting refunds because they illegally overcharged their customers. It is an airline giving rebates to travelers because they have been guilty of unfair competition. It is paying back in full for improperly gained money or property.

But restitution deals with more than property. It is also going back and making things right for hurtful things I've said or done. It's far easier for me to reveal my mustache story than to tell you of the difficult and painful times I've had to ask my wife, my boys, my boss, friends and secretary to forgive me. Restitution is asking forgiveness for harsh words, a quick tongue, or cutting remarks. It is asking forgiveness from a brother you hurt, a mother you caused heartache to, or a former spouse you maligned. Restitution is confessing and seeking forgiveness from an old business partner, neighbor, or roommate. It is admitting my past errors in relationships and humbly seeking forgiveness from the one I've hurt. And it's harder to make personal restitution than property restitution.

Restitution is a discipline in humility. Pride and restitution are incompatible. I'm afraid it's not popular. And it isn't easy. It is one of the most painful disciplines of the obedient life.

But it is biblical. It is the Christian way. Any who seriously seek to follow the teachings of Jesus Christ will walk the painful restitution path at times. Serious followers of the Master will hunger for an easily convicted, tender heart. They will thirst for a soft, easily pricked conscience. And they will act on these promptings, returning to the offended party to make things right. It is the Christian way.

Why Make Restitution?

What would possess a Christian to take such humiliating steps? Why have believers through history practiced this discipline? Are there any good reasons to put yourself through such a torturous experience? Yes. Here are *seven good reasons to make restitution:*

1. It's a matter of obedience. More than fifteen times the Old Testament teaches restitution for followers of God. Jesus confirmed the idea in the New Testament, even recognizing restitution as one of the evidences that "salvation has come to this house" (Luke 19:9). Not that making restitution can save a man or woman. Nothing we can do will bring salvation, except trusting Christ. But the Bible expects restitution to be the kind of thing you do if you follow God. It's consistent with all other teaching in Scripture. The reason we don't like it is not because it's unbiblical; it is because *restitution is in total opposition to our pride.* We hate to be humbled, embarrassed, humiliated. It goes against our nature. So, we would rather save our pride than make restitution. But the Word stands unrevised by our tardiness in obedience. The single best reason to make restitution is because God said to do it. It is a matter of obedience (John 14:15).

2. Restitution reinforces personal happiness. Obedience brings happiness – not a silly, frivolous kind of giddiness, but a deep-seated joy of knowing we are living up to what we've been commanded to do. We may have asked God to forgive us of theft or an interpersonal injustice and He has fully washed it away. Then why do we still feel guilty?

It is horizontal guilt and not vertical guilt from God. We continue to sense a sort of unresolved blame from others.

When we leave a restitution unmade we add a load of guilt to the burdens of our daily walk. We feel guilty. Once we've made wrongs right, that load of horizontal guilt is lifted. We try to shoo our unmade restitutions into the dark recesses of our minds, but they will fly up periodically like nighttime bats from a cave. Once restitution is made we experience a new happiness and freedom in our lives. Then we wonder why we took so long to do it. You'll be a happier (and holier) person after you've made restitution.

3. Restitution releases you to greater service. Unmade restitutions are like a great monkey on your back. Satan sidles up to your ear every time you try to do something for God. He whispers, "Where do you think you're going . . . we know what kind of person you are, remember how you . . ."

Take witnessing for instance. I know one fellow who is absolutely terrified of doing door-to-door soul-winning in the town where he lives. He has swindled so many people that he fears they'll say, "Who are *you* to be telling us about God?" When restitutions are all made, there is a new boldness to serve Christ in other areas.

4. Restitution removes another's stumbling block. Has it occurred to you that another person may hold a grudge against you for what you said or did long ago? Have you ever thought the offended person may be sour, bitter, and full of resentment over a "little thing" you did? To be sure, they are sinning. But aren't you an "accessory" to their sin? Are you providing the opportunity for them to continue in sin? What would happen if you approached them to ask humbly for their forgiveness? What if they granted forgiveness to you? Could they hold a grudge any longer? Your tardiness in making restitution may be placing a great stumbling block in another person's path toward God.

5. Restitution releases you to teach others. If you needed to advise another believer on the advantages of restitution, what story would you tell? My dad told me an unforgettable story of how among his tools he found a hatchet owned by the Church district where he had served years before. He told me how he rationalized it at first, but eventually sent it back to the new district superintendent. He could have taught 200 verses on restitution to me and it would not have moved me as much as his own personal story of an "unburied hatchet."

What story will you tell your children or your grandchildren? Do you have one? Have you never done anything deserving restitution? Not once? After you've made restitution for past wrongs, God often uses these experiences to help you teach others. Perhaps He is having difficulty restoring this discipline to the church because He has so few examples to use.

6. Restitution humbles you. Perhaps this humbling is more than any other discipline of the Christian walk. And any time we are humbled – reminded of who and what we are – it's good!

7. Restitution vaccinates the offended against future wrongs. Nothing can guarantee you won't slip and fall again, but restitution comes close. The next time you are tempted to take something which doesn't belong to you, you will remember the past pain and humiliation of returning to make restitution. When you are about to let loose with a biting, sarcastic, hurtful remark you may think of the embarrassment in store for you when you later must ask this person to forgive you. These thoughts tend to be "preventative medicine." A little pain now –

doing without or biting your tongue – is preferable to the greater pain of restitution.

How to Make Restitution Wisely

Doing the right thing the wrong way may make things worse. Just as there is a collective wisdom about how to pray, read the Bible, or restore a backsliding brother, so there is sound, sensible advice on how to make restitution. If you go about restitution right, you will:

1. Start with the key unmade restitution. What is the thing God is pointing out to you? Don't try to copy other people's stories. Seek God first. He will impress on you where you should begin. It is sometimes the "biggest one." At other times it will be something minor. Seek His face: find out from Him where to begin. Don't be discouraged by the length of your list. Simply deal with one offense at a time. Many Christians have felt released by God after they've worked only part way through their list. Turn to God and ask Him to tell you *where* to begin. Then start *there.*

Perhaps a word of caution is in order about becoming obsessed with restitution. While it is an important discipline of the Christian life, it is not the exclusive one. If you have sought God's guidance and made a list, and are moving toward settling these past accounts, happily march on your way. God is not an angry ogre in the sky who wants to beat you over the head with your unfinished list. He simply wants you to get moving on the road of obedience (1 John 1:7).

2. Prepare your speech. Think through what you are going to say (Luke 15:17-19). Identify the basic offense. Was it harshness? A critical spirit? Disloyalty? Did you steal something? Would you call it unkindness, vengefulness, anger? Was it an outburst of rage? Label it clearly with one or two words. Then make up your speech. Say something like: *"I was wrong in my   (fill in the blank) toward you, and I ask you to forgive me; will you forgive me?"* That's it, just a simple statement of confession and request. Anything more and you're liable to cause more problems than you solve.

And, if you're having trouble saying, "I was wrong," since they were wrong too, remember you are not affirming that they were right. You are simply asking forgiveness for the wrong that *you* are liable for. Their wrongdoing is *their* problem, not yours. So think through what you want to say carefully and prayerfully.

3. Pick the right time, place, and means. Think through the best time to ask. Don't ask when the other person is exceptionally busy, tired, or irritable. Generally, the sooner the better, but don't be so hasty that you pick a poor time and place. Probably you should make restitution privately or at least off to the side of a group. Certainly you should limit the restitution to the offended parties.

A friend once told me of a young man who had taken advantage of a certain young lady. He felt so guilty that he decided to make restitution for his sin by confessing it to his whole residence hall devotional group. The girl soon transferred to another college. This was a foolish restitution. Restitution needs to be no more public than the sin. In fact I believe that direct restitution should not be made at all for past sexual sins. Gaining a clear conscience from God, perhaps making amends to another person as representative (such as a minister or counselor) is probably a better plan.

But, in most cases, direct restitution should be made. A note sometimes works fine, though seldom for a serious matter. A phone call, with the possibility of interchange, is usually better. A face-to-face encounter is often the best means. Use your head, get some advice from a Christian you respect, and do what seems best.

4. Don't combine witnessing with restitution. Simply make your restitution and get on with life. If they inquire, answer their questions. Otherwise, don't advertise how spiritual you are now that you've come back to make things right. Restitution is not a soul-winning method. Occasionally mixing the two will work. Usually it will backfire, ruining both your restitution and your witness.

5. Give a full confession. Come clean. Humans are always trying to make themselves look better, even while making restitution. For instance, we sometimes say, "You know, I've been thinking of how *we* were wrong when . . ." This way you both share the blame. Don't implicate anyone else; just say, "I was wrong; will you forgive me?" Don't say, "I apologize," either. You apologize for minor misunderstandings and comments. When you were wrong say, "I was wrong; will you forgive me?" How easy it is to reduce the seriousness of our offense. Also, avoid saying, "I'm sorry." Of course you're sorry. So are they and everyone else — that the whole thing happened. Being sorry is not enough. Simply say, "I was wrong; will you forgive me?"

Perhaps the easiest way of all to make a partial restitution is to say, "I didn't mean to . . ." When using this phrase we are really saying, "I'm such a nice person I would never imagine hurting another creature; my motives were absolutely pure, yet you were still offended, so out of the goodness of my heart I am coming to confess to you that I didn't mean anything at all." Nonsense! The offended person can't judge your motives. They were offended by your actions, not your motives. So say, "I was wrong; will you forgive me?"

We rebel against this discipline of restitution. Even after you've decided to do it, there is a tendency for self-protection and pride to creep in. But, with some good sense, sound advice, and a commitment to obey Christ in this matter, we can find the happiness of obedient living if we will determine to do it.

Restitution Life-Style

Ideally we're not supposed to be making lists for things we've done in the past. I think God wants us to keep our accounts short. When someone has something against us, we should go and make it right immediately – even if we stand at a sacred altar offering up a holy sacrifice (Matt. 5:23-24). Ideally, as soon as we sense we have hurt someone we should return to them and make things right. The moment we recognize something we don't own is among our things we should return it at once. This is a restitution life-style . . . settling accounts immediately. After all, that's when it's easiest.

However, is this restitution life-style the ideal? Maybe not. Actually God's ideal is not needing to make restitution at all. It is making sure we never take things that are not our own. This is the ideal. The ideal is growing in maturity to the extent we don't even say or do anything which hurts another person. This is the ideal. Certainly we can never be free from misunderstanding, even from having enemies. (Didn't Jesus experience this?) And we can't be guaranteed that a person will even grant their forgiveness. (If we have asked properly with the right attitude, we are free from then on.) But we do know this: we need not be doomed to a life of constant stumbling and falling, regularly doing things which require restitution. God's plan of transformation is far greater than this. To start with, we may need to clean up some past offenses. Then we may need to learn to keep our accounts short through a "restitution life-style." But eventually God wants to bring us to the place where we don't even need to make restitution . . . for we have obeyed Christ completely. For this day we all hunger and thirst.

Now what about you, my friend?

Can you think of any unmade restitutions? Are there things you took that were not yours? Are there people you've hurt who have something against you? Do you have a totally clear conscience?

Bible Study

1. Exodus 22:1-8. What restitutions were the Old Testament people required to make for each of the following offenses:
— Killing or stealing a sheep (22:1).

— An ox (22:1).

— Damage done accidentally through a spreading fire or loose stock (22:5, 6).

2. Leviticus 6:1-5. Most people make restitution on the basis of a 1:1 ratio. However, what is the requirement here? Why?

3. Leviticus 5:16. Is there any application of this principle to the "holy things" of today? What would these things be? To what do you think the 20% penalty clause might apply?

4. Numbers 5:5-8. There may be a restitution you ought to make, but it is no longer possible to find the offended person or organization. In this case a person might make the restitution to a "close relative" as a representative of the aggrieved person. But, if one could not even locate a close relative, to whom is he to make restitution?

5. Deuteronomy 22:13-19. Most popular thinking about restitution relates only to property rights. In this section of scripture there is an enlarging of the idea of restitution to what other area?

6. Luke 19:1-9. Tax collectors during the time of Jesus were a hated lot. The Roman system of revenue collection provided for independent tax collectors and chief collectors who bid for the "business" in their region. They frequently charged far more than the legitimate rates keeping the extra for themselves. Zacchaeus was chief among this despicable lot and had likely cheated many of his fellows over the years. Upon meeting Jesus his heart was burdened by his past wrongs, and he determined to make things right. His restitution was two-fold: both general and specific.

— What *general restitution* did he make (vs. 19:8a)?

— Why might Zacchaeus have made this general restitution?

43

- To what *specific restitution* did he commit (vs. 19:8b)?

- How does Zacchaeus' specific restitution compare with what the law required for financial fraud in Leviticus (Lev. 6:5)?

- What was the observation which Jesus made upon hearing these declarations?

7. *Matthew 5:23-24.* The importance of praise and worship is vital to the Christian. To the Jew it was especially important. Offering a gift up on the altar was the supreme act of devotion and duty. Few would imagine any higher duty.

- However, which activity does Jesus prefer here: worship or interpersonal restitution?

- Does this principle apply when a brother is holding something against you *unjustifiably?*

8. *Personal application* – Is God convicting you about a restitution you need to make? Is there something you took, or an offense you inflicted which you sense God would have you make right? Be careful to avoid working up something on your own. And don't attempt to copy another person's restitution story. The question is what is *God* saying to you? If He is prompting you about some areas, list them in the following space. If God is tenderly tapping on the door of your conscience, don't ignore His gentle prodding. If you never make a list, you'll probably never make the restitutions either. Is there

something you ought to make right? List those candidates for restitution here. If they are private matters, use some sort of code or abbreviations which only you understand, or even use another sheet of paper.

9. Personal Reflection. What is one thing you could and should do in response to the truths you have discovered in this chapter?

— An action to take:

— A promise to make:

3

GRUDGES:
Forgiving Old Hurts

For if you forgive men when they sin against you, your heavenly Father will also forgive you. But if you do not forgive men their sins, your Father will not forgive your sins.

—Matthew 6:14-15

Miss Culp was a stout woman about four and a half feet high. Miss Culp was my third-grade teacher. She led a one-woman crusade to reform education in the city where I grew up. She believed the young teachers were too soft on children. Discipline, harshness, and severity were her methods.

I was a special problem for Miss Culp. Not because I misbehaved so much, but for other reasons. The first was that I passed into third grade from

Miss Hinchman's second-grade room. These two women represented the opposite extremes of educational philosophy. Miss Hinchman's second grade was a womb of positive affirmation. To Miss Hinchman, everything was beautiful, fantastic, lovely, and creative. She believed, "If you expect the best from children, they'll live up to your expectations."

On the other hand, Miss Culp subscribed to the theory, "If you give 'em an inch, they'll take a mile." She believed it was her personal calling to straighten out the rascals Miss Hinchman's softness had produced before we turned out to be juvenile delinquents.

But I had a second problem with Miss Culp. It had to do with my dad. On the first day of class each of us were forced to stand erect, pronounce our name, and tell what our father did for a living. Fearfully I gave my name and announced that my dad was a preacher. "Hurrumph!" she said. "Preachers' kids are the worst of all. I'll be watching out for you." So Miss Culp expected the worst from me. I'm afraid she got it.

But there was a third problem: spelling. Miss Culp gave oral spelling tests. Each student was sent to the front of the room, to stand at attention with "arms straight at your side, fingers pointing to the floor." Miss Culp would retire to the back of the classroom, settling down on a large table she kept back there. She would call off the spelling words for each victim, ordering them to spell each aloud.

I remember my first such experience. "All right young man, spell 'elephant,'" she announced as if she were making an accusation. "E-l-e-p-h . . . h . . ." "Hurry, lad, finish quickly, you either know it or you don't," she said, with no sympathy for my slowness. "E-l-e-p-h . . . e-n-t," I quickly finished. "Wrong" her voice boomed out across the room, with a hint of victory. "No, no, no, that's wrong, try again."

My heart was beating like a pile driver. My

throat was thick and dry. Blood rushed to my face and my flesh turned pink, then red with embarrassment. "E-l-a-p-h-e-n-t," I sputtered out through nervous lips, hoping I might hit it right this time – anything to escape this painful embarrassment and be seated. "Nooooo!" she said scornfully, "You're spelling it worse every time . . . what's the matter with you?"

What was the matter with me, I wondered. Maybe I really was dumb, at least in spelling. I dreaded spelling day every week, I think it was Thursdays. Several times I tried feigning an upset stomach to get out of going to school. It seldom worked. Week after week I was subjected to public reproach and Miss Culp's chiding denouncements for my stupidity in spelling.

I don't remember if I ever spelled "elephant" correctly. I do know that I missed most of the words served up to me from her pitcher's mound in the back of the room. I had been so humiliated in my stupidity that I simply decided "I can't spell." I can still visualize my first red mark on my report card – big red indelible ink – a failure in spelling. This failing grade confirmed my dullness.

At first, I assumed I was the problem. But later, as I realized what she had done to me, I resented her treatment of me. Poor spelling was an ever-present monkey on my back. All through elementary school, high school, and college it was a constant humiliation. I remember one research paper on the millennium I turned in during seminary. I had spelled "millennium" wrong more than sixty times, and I hadn't even been consistent!

I blamed Miss Culp for ruining my attitude about spelling. My resentment grew into a full-blown grudge by high school. Bitterness set in. I never spoke of my third-grade experience to anyone, but I secretly hated Miss Culp for what she had done. "She had no right to treat me that way."

Funny how a little injustice, if nursed, will grow

up to be a full-fledged grudge. I never saw Miss Culp after the fourth grade, but I remembered and resented her. I left her life, but she never left mine. She was constantly haunting me every time I tried to write on a chalkboard or an overhead projector. Worst of all, she was there when I prepared a manuscript for publication. Her memory constantly reminded me of my stupidity in spelling.

Why did she shadow me so? Because of my grudge. Forgive her? Not on your life! "I could never forgive her," I told myself. "She was wrong!"

Sixteen years later I finally got free of Miss Culp's dark shadow. I had been elected as my denomination's Executive Editor of Curriculum, a post in which spelling was a necessity. "Why can't I spell?" I asked myself. "Am I really stupid?" God gently reminded me of my buried feelings toward Miss Culp. I was using her as an excuse for my continued failure to spell accurately. I didn't even look up words when unsure. I figured, "Let the secretary look it up, I can't spell anyway."

As God exposed the breadth and depth of my old grudge against Miss Culp, I came to realize its fruitlessness. I hadn't hurt her a bit. She probably died long ago. In my attempt to even the score with her, I had only hurt myself. The blame for my inability to spell hung like an albatross around my neck, not hers.

I confessed to a sinful grudge that day and fully forgave Miss Culp. No, I did not say she was a fine teacher – she wasn't. But I determined that I would no longer hold a grudge against her. It was too costly to me – I fully forgave her.

Following that incident, I went about learning how to spell. In a few years I caught up. Except when I tell this story, I have almost forgotten about Miss Culp. And, now I can spell.

The Trouble with Grudges

If we slow down and reflect a few moments, each of us will come to admit that a grudge is an awful blot on our soul. What do we gain? Why not release our grudge now? Have you been hurt deeply? Ever? By whom? Has this personal injustice ignited resentment in your heart? Has your resentment turned into a grudge? If so, think about these consequences of a grudge.

1. Grudges don't work. When someone hurts us, we are inclined to settle the score, get even. If we do not forgive the offender the choice remaining is to try revenge, or decide to hold a grudge. Revenge is an outward attempt to even the score. A grudge is revenge turned inward. But a grudge doesn't work. The person who hurt us may not even know how angry and bitter we feel. In fact, they may go on their merry way, completely oblivious to our feelings of resentment. They are happy. We are angry, sour, bitter. The irony: In getting even with another, we hurt ourselves – spiritually and emotionally, perhaps even physically.

2. A grudge grows like cancer. Inner resentment is a spreading cancer of the soul. It multiplies its malignant tentacles, spreading to the deepest parts of our heart. A grudge pours its corrosive bitterness into our entire mindset. Soon we open the door for envy, malice, jealousy, bitterness, gossip, and slander – we will stop at nothing to even the score. Holding a grudge will eat at your insides. Eventually you will become a bitter person. All this happens because you refuse to forgive the one who hurt you. The price is too high. It's not worth it.

3. Grudges generate guilt. If you have a grudge, yet willfully and continually refuse to forgive the one who hurt you, you won't feel forgiven yourself. People who hold grudges seldom sense that God is satisfied with them. You will experience "free-floating guilt," attaching itself to all kinds of little things in your life. You will not be able to put your finger on it, but for some reason or another you feel guilty. You think God is mad at you. You'll never feel fully forgiven and accepted by God. Why? Because it is a universal law: Those who will not forgive, do not feel forgiven.

It is not that God makes some sort of deal with you . . . as if you can buy your forgiveness from God by forgiving others. Jesus Christ has already bought your forgiveness. However, you can inhibit your ability to sense God's forgiveness – by holding a grudge. So, if you often feel that God "has something against me," you may need to look to your past. Have you not forgiven someone who has hurt you deeply? After all "it is in pardoning, that we are pardoned."

4. A grudge handcuffs you to the past. Holding a grudge keeps life running on rewind. You keep looking over your shoulder at some past injustice you experienced. You recall how awful it was. A grudge handcuffs you to this negative past, causing you to blame your present failures on past misfortunes. "If only they hadn't done that, then I'd not be in this jam now. . . ."

Releasing this grudge brings happiness. I remember the joy of one woman who had finally released her grudge against her father. He had sexually abused her as a child. She was 66 years old. Her face radiated, as she bubbled, "For the first time in my life I feel really free! I allowed this thing to ruin my school years, distort my marriage, and sour my old age. Now it is off my back, and I feel such joy . . . so happy . . . so free. If only I had done this years ago."

5. A grudge is an energy leak. The embers of

a grudge require tending. Resentment left to itself flickers and dies out. It must be fed to be kept alive. Where does this fuel come from? It comes from your own mental and emotional energies. Carrying a grudge pokes holes in your energy bucket. You will feel constantly tired, weary, and lethargic. Fatigue is the faithful companion of a grudge. At the end of each day you will collapse in exhaustion, wondering why you feel so fatigued. It is because you are wasting great amounts of unconscious energy maintaining your grudge. Releasing this grudge through forgiveness will result in a brand-new surge of emotional and physical energy.

This is not to say that everyone who is tired at the end of a hard day's work is harboring a grudge. Weariness is a symptom of an unforgiving spirit, just as a rash is a symptom of poison ivy. All rashes do not indicate poison ivy, but a person infected with poison ivy will have a rash. All exhaustion does not indicate a buried grudge, but if you've got a grudge, there is a good chance you'll experience fatigue.

6. A grudge usurps God's rightful role. The ultimate sin in an unforgiving spirit is that we take God's authority from Him. God, and God alone, has the right to condemn men and women. Only God has the right to hold another accountable for sin. Vengeance is His exclusive domain. When we refuse to forgive another we raise ourselves to the level of God, as if we can hold another under charges for their sin. Forgiveness allows us to turn this account over to the ultimate Collector of debts.

Insufficient Remedies for a Grudge

All of us recognize the danger of grudges. This leads us to somehow try to remedy the problem. One danger is to choose an insufficient remedy – treating only the surface problem, not the deep resentment within. Consider these inadequate remedies:

1. Cover it over. You won't escape the clutches of a grudge by simply trying to cover it over. This kind of suppression will only lead to a further poisoning of your spirit. Saying, "I'll pretend it never happened," would be like trying to cure cancer with aspirin. Covering up a grudge with soothing words will only submerge it, allowing it to spread unchecked inside you. Radical surgery is the need, not aspirin!

2. Forget it. God is not asking you to forget the offense. You simply can't do it. He does – but He does not ask you to do the same. He has designed you so that your memory contains all the events of your life. It is conceivable that you could remember everything that ever occurred in your life. You can especially remember painful experiences, or more so the feelings resulting from these experiences.

When you fully forgive a person, you do not have the capacity to forget their sin. "Forgive and forget" is an ability beyond human capacity.

While you can't forget an offense, you can choose not to dwell on it. When the devil brings it up again, you can quickly dismiss the event as forgiven. You can't fully erase the memory banks of your mind. God won't do it for you. But you do have the power to refuse to think on past injustices, once forgiven. The curious thing is that once an offense is fully forgiven, the time between your remembering it will increase as time passes. Eventually months, even years, will pass without a thought of this deep hurt. For all practical purposes you might say, "I've forgotten it," though it still lies deep in your memory. The difference: that file is now marked "forgiven."

3. Excuse it. "But she was wrong," I argued

with the Lord about my Miss Culp. "If I forgive her it would be like admitting what she did was all OK." No. God doesn't ask me to justify a person's sin – only He can do that. He only asks me to forgive them. We misunderstand forgiveness. Forgiveness can only be granted if the other person was wrong. Fascinating thought: it is only in being wronged that I am empowered to forgive. To forgive Miss Culp I had to label her actions wrong, I could not excuse them.

God calls us to forgive one another as God forgave us (Col. 3:13). How did God handle your sins? Did He dismiss them with a hasty "Oh, you needn't worry about your sins, they're minor and I understand"? No. God forgives us by condemning our sins, then granting a pardon. This is what He asks you to do. Condemn the injustice as wrong, then grant a pardon anyway. Hate the sin, but love the sinner enough to forgive him or her!

So what about you, my friend?

Have you been hurt? Has someone been unjust to you? A parent? Brother or sister? Child? Neighbor? Teacher? Former spouse? Perhaps a group or institution hurt you: a school, church, committee, board, youth group. Have you fully forgiven these people? Do you harbor a bit of a grudge for anyone anywhere in your past?

If so, you can get this monkey off your back for good today! You can decide that from this hour forward you are marking that debt "paid in full." It is in the willing to forgive that you can actually forgive. You can do it. You can! In one single transaction you can determine that you will no longer consider that your offender has an "outstanding balance" with you. The debt is "history" . . . cancelled . . . paid in full – turned over to the Eternal Debt Collector. Not because they were right, but simply because you want to obey Christ and please the Fa-

55

ther. He has commanded that you forgive others as His Father forgave you. How was that? Completely, wholly, irrevocably. Can you do the same for another now? It's not a question of who's right; it's a question of what's right.

Perhaps your injury was especially deep. Could you at least begin to forgive? Are you telling yourself "I can't forgive" when you really mean "I won't forgive?" Are you truly unable to forgive? Are you willing to be made willing? Is the Lord gently urging you to begin? To start? If so, why not turn the corner today? Why not tell Him right now, "Lord, I'm going to begin my road to recovery . . . and I shall not turn back until I have fully forgiven that person." The Great Forgiver will help you.

Bible Study

1. Matthew 18:21-35.

  — What was the question posed which brought up the subject of forgiveness (verse 21)?

  — What does each of the following parts of the parable represent to you?
  • The King

  • The first servant

  • The hopeless debt

  • The king's cancellation of the debt

- The fellow servant

- The fellow servant's debt

— Strictly speaking, many Bible scholars feel a parable essentially tries to teach only one point. Based on verse 35 what do you think that point is?

2. *Matthew 6:12-15.*

— What should we pray to God for (verse 12)?

— What example of forgiveness do we want God to use in forgiving us (verse 12)?

— What promise do you see here (verse 14)?

— What warning do you see (verse 15)?

3. *James 2:12-13.*

— What is the positive Christian characteristic of being forgiving mentioned here?

— What warning is repeated again here?

4. *Colossians 3:13.*

— What example are we to use in forgiving others?

5. *Luke 23:33-34.*

— Based on this example, how would you answer the question "How far should you go with this forgiveness thing?"

6. *Personal Reflection.*

What is one single thing you could do in response to the truths of this chapter?

— An action to take:

— A promise to make:

4

THOUGHT LIFE:
Overcoming Impure Thoughts

And we take captive every thought to make it obedient to Christ.
—2 Corinthians 10:5

We live in a sex-saturated society. Advertisers use "sex appeal" to sell perfume, shave lotion, blue jeans, hosiery, even toothpaste. Most of the TV advertising we see is carefully designed to appeal to our sensual natures. A modern diet cola advertisement is quite as erotic as many "girlie magazines" of a few decades ago. Magazines, books, newspapers, billboards, movies, even office conversations offer stimulation of the sexual parts of our beings. An increasing host of "soft-core" TV programs titillate millions of viewers nightly, and what was once considered blatantly "sexy" is now accepted as good taste in clothing.

Is it any wonder that believers living in such a society are troubled by improper sexual thoughts? The temptation to dwell on sexual themes and erotic thoughts is everywhere.

Impure thoughts are not a temptation limited to young men. I once thought this to be so, but experience in counseling many years has taught me otherwise. I have talked with scores of older men who are plagued with this private sin and have suffered for the forty or fifty years since their teen years. Neither is lust the exclusive sin of men. My wife reports from her traveling and speaking schedule that she has counseled with innumerable women, young and old alike, who suffer with habitual sensual fantasies.

If this area of temptation is completely foreign to you, or you are aghast that Christians exist who wrestle with this awful demon, the following excerpts from two letters, may be helpful in describing the depth of this particular fleshly sin:

> "I'm desperate for any help you can give me. I am so sick of my obsession with impure thoughts that I've even thought of suicide. I feel so filthy, so dirty, so unworthy after I've given in and dwelled on some memory or daydream about a beautiful woman. My guilt brings me to confess. And I promise God I'll never do it again. But I do. I always do. Sometimes I fight heroically. Sometimes I even beat this monster, but I often fall. *Real* often.
>
> "Is there help for me? Am I too far gone? Should I simply give up at trying to be a Christian? That's how I feel sometimes. This filthy habit has clung to my life for more than 30 years. I've never told anybody else about it. My pastor, the board, the whole church – even my

wife – all think I am a perfect model Christian. But I know I am rotten inside. I feel like such a hypocrite! Is there hope for me? If so, I need it soon."

Or, consider this letter my wife received from a delightfully talented woman.

"I had never even thought of how women have impure thoughts until last week at your session. I always figured guys were the ones who had problems with 'dirty thoughts.' But maybe I have a problem too.

"There's this handsome young man in our church choir who is not only talented, but pays attention to *me*. My husband is one of those guys who pretty well ignores me – especially in public. But this guy treats me like a queen. He listens to what I have to say, looks right into my face, and acts like I am an important person. You know what I mean . . . he just treats me *special*.

"Anyway, I wonder if this has become a trap for me. I think about him all the time . . . while I'm working, during church services, even when I'm with my husband. Not that I think of having sex with him or anything like that. I just invent those intensely romantic scenes in my mind, as if they are happening between this fellow and me. It's exciting! But I wonder if it's wrong. Is it OK as long as I don't actually fantasize about the actual sex act? I hope you can guide me on this because I've been troubled about it all this week.

"P.S. All this has made a big difference in how I feel about myself lately. I now have something to get up for in the morning again. Even my husband complimented me recently (believe it or not!) on how nicely I've been dressing. Could these thoughts be wrong when they seem to have so many benefits????"

What would *you* tell this woman? What would you tell that man?

What is "Lust"?

Some spiritual advisors are not worried by these kinds of thoughts. They soothe troubled Christians by saying that sexual fantasies are common, normal and quite innocent. A few even consider impure thoughts as healthy for your marriage.

The Bible is not so soft. It names such thoughts with one word: "lust." God's Word condemns lust as sin. Christians are to get rid of it along with other evil thoughts, words, and actions. Fooling around with lust is like playing with a loaded gun. Given the chance, impure thoughts will ruin your soul. Lust is serious. Jesus shocked His audience by stating that in God's sight, lust is as serious as adultery itself.

So, what is lust? It is dwelling on sexual thoughts which, if you carried them out in real life would be clearly sin. Lust is sexual or sensual fantasies about someone you are not married to. Lust is sinful sexual passion. It is sinful sexual thinking nurtured in your mind and dwelled on for the sake of personal sensual pleasure. Lust is willful – is purposefully thinking these thoughts.

Lust is not temptation. If you are blessed with high sexual energy, you may be especially tempted in this area. Satan may frequently remind you of some memory, tempting you to dwell on it. Or he may attempt to seduce you to fantasize about a particular person. This is not lust; it is temptation. While it is sometimes difficult for us to determine that fine line between disobedience and temptation, there is a world of difference between an evil thought and the thought of evil. Even our Perfect Example had thoughts of evil while He was not guilty of evil thoughts. He banished these thoughts from His mind with a decisive refusal to surrender, and a quote from God's word. Lust is not temptation. It is *surrendering* to temptation . . . dwelling on the impure thoughts Satan has presented to our minds.

Neither is dreaming lustful in itself. Dreams are a mysterious function of our subconscious mind. Have you ever dreamed that you had shot and killed someone? I have. I woke up trembling, and *felt* as if I had actually committed murder. But I was not guilty of murder, even in God's sight. God does not hold us accountable for the mysterious working of our subconscious mind. Dreaming is not sin . . . *day*dreaming is the problem.

Lust is purposefully dwelling on sinful, sensual thoughts. These are the wild horses of our mind which must be tracked down, captured, and made obedient to Christ.

So What's the Trouble with Impure Thoughts?

1. You will come to justify sin. The Great Deceiver tells you, "Don't worry about these thoughts, they're harmless, innocent fantasies." He would like you to dismiss them as the ordinary musings of all humanity. This sometimes works. The human mind cannot survive long when our behavior is out of sync with our beliefs. If you believe something is wrong you will want to stop it. However, if you fail at your attempt to stop, you will then try to sanctify the thought, word, or action. You justify it as appropriate, thus escaping the tension of doing what you know you shouldn't. If you do not beat this thing, eventually you'll simply justify lust as ordinary and inescapable.

2. You will live a double life. If you are truly saved, the Holy Spirit won't abandon His convicting work. Though you tell yourself this sin is okay, the Holy Spirit will keep telling you otherwise. You will then adopt a new strategy: you partition life like a rolltop desk. You decide to simply ignore this *part* of your life. You create a pigeonhole for impure thoughts and pretend they don't exist.

Churches are full of men and women who live this kind of double life. They tuck their evil thoughts into a sealed desk drawer of their mind. Into this drawer they enter alone. These folk seem quite ordinary when you meet them, work with them, or serve on a committee with them. But they are a Jekyll-Hyde Christian. Though they grow in other areas, appearing to make progress along the highway of holiness, they have a cancerous closet in their mind. These double-minded Christians sneak off to the private closets of their minds. There they dwell on corrupt and sordid thoughts, then cower back full of guilt and despair. This is a wretched way to live.

3. Lustful thirst is unquenchable. Sexual pursuits outside marriage are like an empty well. They promise satisfaction but leave you unfulfilled. It is an unsatisfying pursuit. The more you dwell on these thoughts, the less exciting they will be for you. In your quest for fulfillment you will mount a perpetual treadmill of self-gratification. The faster you chase satisfaction, the less satisfied you'll be. Like drinking salt water, the more you drink the less satisfied you'll be.

4. You will become obsessed. Sexual fantasies are addictive. Once you establish the habit, you will begin a relentless cycle of obsession. These thoughts will gradually permeate every recess of your mind. They will dominate you, enslaving you in a bondage of despair. Eventually your entire life will be tarnished by them. You will be "hooked" on the opium of sexual fantasies. You will be obsessed with your quest for satisfaction – always hungering, never satisfied. You will then be lust's slave.

5. Lust diverts wholesome sexual energy. The devil didn't invent sex. God did. He termed it "good" along with the rest of creation. *The most important sex organ in your body is your mind.* God designed your mind with the powerful capacity to direct and focus sexual energy toward another. This remarkable mental ability is God-given and designed to produce the great sexual satisfaction in marriage. This God-given ability should be focused on your mate, not squandered on some fleeting fantasy. When you surrender to impure thoughts, you poke a leak in your own sexual energy, which ultimately produces frustration and unfulfillment.

6. Thoughts lead to action. On this one concept philosophers and great thinkers throughout history agree: as you think, you shall become. If you think positive, uplifting, wholesome, healthy thoughts, you will eventually become a positive, healthy, uplifting person. If you think gloomy, negative, sickly thoughts, you will turn out to be a negative, sickly person. What we think, we become. As Jesus put it, "As a man thinketh in his heart, so is he."

Your mind is like a fertile field. A field doesn't care what you plant in it – corn, oats, or wheat. It simply obeys the universal law: what you plant in the field, you'll get back in abundance. If you plant corn, you'll get corn, plant wheat, you'll get wheat, and so on. Your mind is like this fertile field. Your thoughts are seeds. What you plant will sprout and grow, eventually producing an abundant crop in real life.

Can you see the ultimate results of impure thinking? "Innocent Fantasies" planted in your mind will eventually produce an abundant crop of *sinful behavior.* What you thought was a benign mental pastime carried on in the privacy of your mind will turn out to be the doorway through which your moral downfall enters. Thoughts lead to actions. Your sensual thought life will not escape this universal law of life. Sooner or later you will act as you think.

Ten Steps Out:

How to Completely Overcome Impure Thoughts

If you have been enslaved by impure thoughts, there is good news for you. You can be free. Completely so! If you seriously hunger to be free from the bondage of impure thoughts, God is able to do it. He can!

The following are ten steps you can begin today. They are not some philosophy dreamed up in an ivory tower of theory. Rather, they have been hammered out in the trenches of life by hundreds of men and women who once suffered in defeat, but are now free of this "clinging" sin (Heb. 12:1-2).

Though they are "steps" in one way, they are not to be considered completely sequential. Though there is a general arrangement of the order, each point must be continually maintained while others are added. Hundreds have followed these steps and found complete victory. You can too!

1. Confess. All improvement starts with confession. Quit dismissing impure thoughts as inconsequential. Tear down the partition to that private closet in your mind, allowing Christ's light to expose these thoughts of darkness. Call them what God does: lust. Agree with God concerning this sin and begin your journey to a pure mind.

2. Expose lust's "big lie." Admit to yourself and to God that this way of life does not bring the ultimate satisfaction. Acknowledge that the promises of the deceiver are out-and-out lies. Lust is not satisfying. It never has been and never will be. Keep reminding yourself that the devil is a liar from the beginning. Start remembering where all this "daydreaming" could eventually lead . . . to sinful behavior, moral collapse, and maybe the break-up of your home.

3. Starve the sources. Track down your stimuli and get tough with them! What is it that gets your mind going? Is it the "story section" of a woman's magazine? Is it a particular TV program? Videos? Soap operas? Music? Is it a certain person who is flirting with you? Is it double-meaning kidding with someone? Is it "girlie magazines"? Do romance novels start your sexual engines? Is it indecent jokes or stories of another's sexual activities? What is the outside source of your temptation?

Your mind is fearfully and wonderfully made. It is incredible. Better than man's best computer, the mind is constantly receiving messages, processing input, and affecting your behavior. When you expose your mind to stimuli, it affects what you think. If your mind is wandering into sexual fantasies, somewhere along the line it has received stimuli which triggered these thoughts. Track down and avoid your besetting stimuli. "Be careful, little eyes, what you see."

If you were a rehabilitated alcoholic, you would have to learn to stay away from alcohol. If God had delivered you from drinking, would you drop into a bar just to check out how well God had delivered you? Would you order a beer and set it before you just to test your resistance? No! You would avoid alcohol in any form whatsoever.

So it is with lust. Lust is a hungry carnivorous monster. It must be fed "flesh" to survive. External stimuli trigger lust. These stimuli continuously nourish and multiply a lustful orientation. Since society is saturated with sexual stimuli, you may be tempted to play along – simply giving up. But you need not do this. With a little thought you could make a list of the ten most dangerous "triggers" for temptation in this area. Then starve the sources.

4. *Win with the Word!* How shall a young man keep his way pure? How will you keep from sinning against God? By hiding God's Word in your heart. A consistent habit of reading, memorizing and meditating on God's Word is incompatible with impure thoughts. One will eventually destroy the other. Which one wins in your life? (Consider Psalm 119:11 . . . better yet, *all* of Psalm 119.)

A believer who is failing to live above impure thoughts will almost always confess he or she is not practicing a regular habit of systematic devotional Bible reading. The road to thought purity always runs through Scripture. The most important habit you can begin, to aid you in your battle against temptation, is a daily "Time Alone with God." If the devil is tempting you to lustful thoughts, start with these scriptures:

2 Corinthians 10:5	Psalms 119:9-11
2 Timothy 2:22	Hebrews 3:1
1 Timothy 5:2	Colossians 3:2-7
Galatians 5:24-25	Philippians 4:7
Psalms 13:2	Psalms 19:13-14
Proverbs 5:1-23	Proverbs 6:24-29
James 1:14-15	1 Corinthians 6:18-20
1 Timothy 4:12	Proverbs 2:12-19
1 Corinthians 10:13	Proverbs 7:1-27

5. *Practice "Displacement."* "An idle mind is the devil's workshop." If you have ample amounts of unoccupied time, you will be a "sitting duck" for Satan. If you are often alone, you may find Satan coming in like a flood during these times. Perhaps your job is boring and unchallenging, allowing time for your mind to wander – and wonder. When a mind is unoccupied the devil takes this opportunity to suggest sinful thoughts for you to dwell on. What you do with his "pitches" will determine your destiny!

Displacement is concentrating your mental energies on other things (cf. Philippians 4:8). It is filling up your brain with other thoughts, focusing your mental powers elsewhere. Impure thoughts are crowded out. Search for a mental infatuation with something else: scripture memorization, baseball, an invention you're working on, taking a class at the nearby college, a new floor plan for your "dream house." Anything decent will do. Find something which can occupy your mind, and displace impure thoughts.

6. Redirect your thoughts. If you are married, you have already discovered that the temptation to impure thoughts does not pass with the wedding ceremony. In some ways it increases. But the married person has one definite counterforce against this temptation: When you are tempted to think sexual thoughts, go ahead and think them. *What?* Yes. Rather than developing a negative obsession about these thoughts, redirect them properly. Where? Toward your mate. Use your sexual thoughts to enhance your own sex life in marriage. Focus your thoughts toward marriage – toward that relationship where sexual expression is beautiful and God-sanctified. This is the wholesome use of your powerful mental sexual energies.

7. "Drink from your own spring." If you are single, skip this one. If you are married, work on developing a satisfying sexual relationship at home. A developing sexual relationship takes tenderness, understanding, and patient hard work. Learn to flirt with each other again. Recapture the tremendous sexual power of that meaningful glance. Practice romance. Spend some money. Surprise him! Allure her! Keep the fire hot at home.

8. Turn temptation into spiritual energy. Do a turnabout on the devil. When he introduces some delectable temptation to you, immediately go to prayer. Not for yourself, but for *others.* Take your temptation as a signal that Satan would love to have you fall so that he can more easily get at those in your circle of influence. What about your son? daughter? people in your church? someone you discipled? spouse? congregation? Could they be tempted likewise? Most likely they are. Thus go to prayer for them, that they will be strong in their similar temptation. This is a great trick to play on Satan. His temptation merely sends you to earnest prayer for others. The more he tempts you, the more you pray – what a clever ploy! What a mighty ministry of intercessory prayer!

9. Become accountable. You will doubtless never beat this one alone. Find someone of the same sex whom you trust, preferably someone who has fought this battle and won. In a few cases I have known of husband-wife accountability on thought life, but often an accountability relationship with someone of the same sex is better. Ask him or her to check up on your thought life every time he or she sees you. Make sure they are tough on you, never satisfied with less than 100% purity.

10. Seek deliverance. This sin is usually too powerful to beat by the first nine steps alone. If you carefully follow each of the above prescriptions you will find great victories and progress in your struggle. You will become an overcomer most of the time. You may say, "I've come a long way," but you are not completely free. You will still yearn for *complete* freedom. You want more than partial victory. You are not even satisfied with 100% "victory." You want *deliverance* (Rom. 7:24-25a; 8:2-3).

You can have it. God carries deliverance in stock. You can do more than fight the battle – often winning, sometimes losing – "one step forward, then two steps backward." You can do more than resist the magnetic pull of the flesh.

True, you will likely not ever be totally delivered

from temptation in this area (or at least related areas). But you need not fall. You need not be content with being a "recovering lustaholic."

You can have *deliverance.* You'll never completely beat this thing through striving, though strive you must. You'll never defeat this clinging habit through hard work, though work you must. Only the "Strong Man" can bind this evil spirit of the mind. *It is only the Son of God who can drive these thieves from the temple of your heart.* God can deliver you. And He will, if you let Him.

Now don't leap too quickly at this opportunity for a shortcut. Don't say to yourself, "Good, I'll seek instant deliverance . . . it's certainly easier than memorizing these Scriptures." God will see through your shallowness and spiritual laziness. He expects you to work. And *as you work,* He also works (Phil. 1:6; 2:13). So, as you pursue thought purity, also seek His total deliverance. He can do it. He has done it for many; He can do it for you!

It could happen today, or after many months or even years of seeking. It could happen gradually or it could occur in a single instant. But it can happen. There is not one sin which you cannot be free of. God forgives. He also delivers. Let it happen!

Now what about you, my friend?

Do you suffer defeat in your thought life? Has lust plagued you for years? Have you almost given up hope of being free of this beast? Don't give in. Don't give up. Rather, cheer up! Look up! Your hope of deliverance is near. If His gentle Spirit convicts you of this sin, rejoice. For He never convicts without the hope of correction. Your conviction is cause for joy. There is hope. Beginning today, you can be free!

Bible Study

1. *Matthew 5:27-29.*

    — In what way does Jesus here expand the interpretation of the seventh commandment?

2. *2 Corinthians 10:4-5.*

    — What *weapons* might Paul be speaking of which can demolish "strongholds" and take "captive thoughts?"

3. *Psalm 119:9-10.*

    — What preventative for sin is prescribed here?

4. *1 Corinthians 10:13.*

    — Is it possible to be in a spot where we are helpless before temptation, unable to have victory?

    — What is the difference between "resistible temptation" and "escapable temptation?"

5. *Colossians 3:5-6.*

    — To what does lust belong?

— What are we told to do with lust?

6. *Philippians 4:7-8.*

— Besides guarding our hearts, what else will the "peace of Christ" guard?

— What are eight types of thoughts with which we should fill our minds?

7. *Colossians 3:1-2.*

— Where are we to set our hearts and minds?

— What can a Christian do to develop a heavenly "mindset?"

8. Personal Reflection.

What is one single thing you could do in response to the truths of this chapter?

— An action to take:

— A promise to make:

5
RESTORATION:
Restoring a Fallen Christian

Brothers, if someone is caught in a sin, you who are spiritual should restore him gently. But watch yourself, or you also may be tempted.

—Galatians 6:1

Suppose someone has taken a spiritual tumble in your church. They have fallen into sin and many know about it. A little group gathers off to the side to discuss the tragedy. One opens the conversation with, "Isn't it just terrible? Of all people, who would ever have suspected *him?*" Another replies, "He should have known better, it was just plain stupid." A third adds, "We've got to hold the whole family up in prayer during this time; you know this was not the *first* time."

So go the unspiritual, fleshly responses to a believer's fall into sin. We have a difficult time dealing with a brother's spiritual failure in the Christian community. If a leader or minister falls, the difficulty is doubled. What's a congregation to do when one of its own falls?

What if one of our unmarried teen women gets pregnant? Or how should we respond when one of the board members is being charged with tax evasion in his business? Or how about a fine fellow in our choir who is being charged by his former wife with molesting his children? What do we do when one of our adult Sunday school teachers separates from his wife and files for a no-fault divorce? What would you do if you caught another Christian secretly meeting someone who is not his or her spouse?

Sometimes Christians fall into sin. It is not the norm, and it should not be expected, but it happens. Christians sometimes stumble and fall. Temptation, like a mighty gust of wind, can sweep a believer off his feet and send him tumbling. When this happens, what should the rest of us do?

We are to restore the fallen brother. We are to help him back on his feet again. This discipline is both personal and corporate . . . the individual has a responsibility as does the entire church. We are commanded to help the brother up. This is restoration.

What *Not* to Do When a Brother Falls

Restoring another Christian is a demanding responsibility; it's a touchy task. How will the person respond? Will they blow up at me? Is the whole thing merely a rumor that I should ignore? It's none of our business anyway, is it? It is indeed our responsibility. God wants to restore the fallen one, and He chooses to use us as His helpers/restorers. The responsibility for restoration lies squarely on the shoulders of other Christians. Yet because of misunderstanding, fear, and lack of training, we often sidestep this command. Instead, we bypass the whole issue when faced with another's sin. We must avoid these popular "cop outs."

1. We must not whitewash sin. Excusing sin as normal or ordinary doesn't help. "After all, he's only human," we say, apparently believing it is simply natural for Christians to fall into sin. Some churches have used the guise of "loving the sinner" to completely ignore the commands of the Scripture. Yes, we must love the sinner, even when he is a fallen brother, but we are not to dismiss his sin with a trivial remark about humanity, treating sin as inconsequential. Jesus told one sinner "Neither do I condemn you," but He quickly added "Go and sin no more" (John 8:11).

Like leaven, sin spreads its influence. Sin is contagious. It spreads from one to another. We are called to restore our fallen brother, not merely excuse him. Whitewashing sin by excusing it as human error bypasses the whole issue, ignores God's command to restore the fallen brother, and gives the would-be restorer an "easy out" from a tough task.

2. We must avoid witch-hunting. The trouble with this Christian discipline of restoring a brother is that those least likely to do it are the best for the job. Conversely, those most likely to greet gleefully the idea of restoring another are the worst ones to do it. In most churches there are a few people who would love the idea of signing up for "search and destroy" missions to uncover and correct the sins of others. They are experts at exposing and condemning sin. These "headhunters" love nothing better than the juicy discovery of some member's wrongdoing. They have what John Calvin called the "spirit of accusation." Like the Pharisees, they are always anxious to cast the first stone. If given their way, they'd return to the days of Salem, Massachusetts, and sensational church trials, placing offenders in stocks or hanging them as witches. Obviously, this kind of a "witch-hunting" atmosphere is not what the discipline of restoration is all about.

3. We must not ignore sin. While most churches may have a witch-hunter or two, most of us are in little danger of such excesses. But we are just as guilty. In our attempt to avoid the excesses we may do worse — simply ignore the whole business altogether, hoping it will go away. We attribute the sin to an exaggerated rumor saying, "It's probably not true anyway." We remain coldly aloof from the sin and the fallen brother, figuring it will evaporate with time. "It's none of our business anyway," we say, hoping that the fallen brother will heal himself, or fade away, or something!

If you had an ugly festering wound on your leg, with obvious red lines creeping up toward your heart, would you ignore it? No. When one of the members in the body of Christ is infected with sin, the rest of us must take action to bring healing, not stand casually by in indifference. Ignoring sin won't make it go away. We are to get involved, take a risk, help out. That's what being a Christian is all about. The local church is a hospital for sinners, not a musty museum for perfect saints.

4. We must not hastily expel the stumbling saint. While we should not overlook sin, we must guard ourselves from rapidly booting the brother or sister out of our fellowship. Some churches pride themselves in their "purity." One pastor bragged to a neighboring pastor with a condescending tone, "We keep a tight reign on our families; not a single one of our people are divorced or separated." The neighboring pastor replied, "Right, when they get divorced, you kick 'em out, and they come over to us."

We don't like to fix our own messes. Sometimes

we send them down the street. But that is what restoration is all about – fixing messes. Kicking a person out is a radical remedy like amputating an infected leg. It is not to be used until all other attempts at restoration fail.

This does not mean that we must never expel people from the fellowship of the church. We must differentiate between the Christian who stumbles and falls into sin, and the one with a deep-seated rebellion who refuses to accept correction. The second live in open rebellion continuing in sin with an obstinate contempt for God. This latter kind – a willful and rebellious sinner living in open disobedience and offering alibis for his defiance – should indeed be expelled. For this situation Paul said, "Expel the wicked man from among you" (1 Cor. 5:13). But, the one who trips and falls, slipping off the straight and narrow road of obedience must be restored, not expelled.

5. We must not practice "shunning." In many churches an offending member is neither restored nor expelled – he is simply given the cold shoulder. He is not officially ignored or rejected; he is just treated with icy politeness. And there is a dark thing happening – a brother or sister, while still present, is being quietly excluded from true fellowship. All interchange is mechanical and automatic. This ostracism is somewhat like the "shunning" practiced by the Amish and other strict sects. We are no better. The person guilty of moral failure never hears his sin spoken of. He is politely greeted and treated civilly. But he is never again included in anything. It is a social excommunication.

Most persons who experience this kind of psychological torture eventually drop out of the church or switch to another fellowship which seems more open and accepting. In fact, in almost every community there are churches which, like the cities of refuge in Israel, are known to provide loving relief and asylum for hurting people. The word gets around. Is your church such a "community of the compassionate?"

How to Restore a Brother

The Bible is so intensely practical. It is more than a book full of theological ideas we are asked to believe. Rather, it is a guidebook for everyday life. The Book tells us specifically what to do when our brother stumbles into sin. We are to "restore" him. The word is the same as used for "mending nets" or for a surgeon "setting a dislocated bone." Restoration means becoming my brother's "repairman." We are to get involved in helping the Christian to his feet again, putting him back where he belongs. Here's how:

1. Someone must face the offender. Restoration is face-to-face work. It should not be done by letter, or with the telephone. The Bible tells us this is work for the spiritual ones among our congregation. It's work for mature Christians. Novices and carnal Christians need not apply. The restorer must pick a time and place to face the brother with the intention of restoring him. Many churches leave this work to the pastor. The Scriptures don't. It's a Christian discipline which all who are spiritual should bear.

Restoration is delicate work. You are attempting to correct the trajectory of a brother or sister who has wandered off. It is not to be done without much prayer and thought. Perhaps this is why so few do it. But if we take the Bible seriously, we who are spiritual, mature, guided by the Spirit, are to set up a meeting face-to-face with the brother who has fallen in order to restore him.

2. Your spirit must be right. The restorer must approach the brother or sister in a spirit of meekness, vividly remembering that he too has feet of clay. He must avoid gossip, and keep his talking and advice to the minimum. Restoring is not lecture-giving. The godly restorer puts the best construction on the actions and motives of the fallen brother. He is not looking for an opportunity to give harsh, heavy-handed condemnation or to illustrate his own spiritual superiority. He is not accusatory nor does he have a holier-than-thou attitude. He is sympathetic and tactful, carefully selecting his words and body language.

Most of all he is humble. Restoration is not the work for those with a spiritual superiority complex. The godly restorer comes, not as one stooping down to raise another up to his level. Rather, he comes alongside as a friend to help a brother back to his feet. Restorers are meek people – a blend of strength and tenderness – strong enough to set the broken bone, yet gentle enough to avoid hurting the patient more than necessary as they do it.

There are precious few folk who meet these criteria. In fact, merely reading the description causes most of us to give up. "Obviously this is not the kind of work for me," we say to ourselves. "I'll pray while others do this restoring business." But we are too hasty in dismissing the power of the Holy Spirit in our lives.

Do you *want* to be this way? Is it your hunger? Can you see a glimmer of hope that you might some day become this sort of a restorer? If so, then let God work in you. If He lays it on your heart to help some slipping (or slipped) saint, then do so without delay. You may discover hidden, untapped characteristics for being just this kind of person. Anyway, how will you know if you never try?

3. The goal is recovery. Restoring is about discipline, not punishment. Punishment looks backward to the offense and seeks to inflict pain. Discipline looks forward towards recovery. Restoring is discipline. Restoring puts a fellow back on course and gets him moving in the right direction again. You do not visit your brother to see him cower in pain and guilt. You want to get the confession out of the way as quickly as possible, so you can get on with bringing the cure.

4. Determine your approach. Before you go, determine what your approach will be. Are you offering simple words to admonish, a more definite correction, or clear-cut rebuke? Each person and each situation, may require a different approach. In most cases, we will be giving gentle admonition saying something like this:

> "What I want to talk to you about is _____. I don't know for sure, and I could be wrong, but I want to offer a gentle nudge to you as my friend about _____. If I'm wrong, forget it and forgive my intrusion. If I'm partly right, then think about it . . . kick it around a bit and see if God is saying the same thing."

There is seldom a need to be more harsh than this. In some instances a more direct correction or outright rebuke is required, but a gentle admonition given earlier is often adequate.

5. The means to recovery is repentance. When a Christian falls there is only one way back – repentance. Repentance is sorrow, brokenness, heartache for sin. It begins with a confession, but leads to a desire to abandon the sin. When a real Christian falls, he experiences plenty of guilt and remorse. He is usually ready to repent. He may have even already repented privately.

That is why it is so important to approach a fallen friend carefully at the most appropriate time. Recently the Lord prompted me to offer correction to a friend about his treatment of a certain individual. I called on Monday and made arrangements for lunch. At lunch that Wednesday, after I had offered the admonition he said, "I knew the moment you called two days ago why you wanted to see me and I've thought about it these last two days." God had already prepared his heart to receive the word of correction. Restorers never arrive first. The Holy Spirit gets there first.

Occasionally, however, a person will not receive the correction at all. Sometimes the individual will deny everything, even attack you. He may dismiss it as a minor offense, tell you it has been exaggerated, or offer excuses for the behavior. Sometimes this happens even after you have done everything right. If it does, simply offer an apology for offending the person and change the subject. Dismiss the issue, and treat the person tenderly and carefully. Remember, a fallen Christian has a serious spiritual wound. Sometimes when you offer therapy, it causes greater pain than the wound itself. In these cases, simply withdraw and let the Holy Spirit continue His work.

Immediate rejection may, however, be only a temporary delay. Sometimes your admonition is rejected, only to become an embryo for eventual obedience. The following excerpts from a letter illustrate just such a response.

"I've always had a good marriage, or at least I thought so. But last year at camp I made the acquaintance of a woman serving on staff with me. My wife was home with our little kids, and this woman and I struck up a friendship. We shared lots of interests and liked to talk with each other. Her friendly response to me was a powerful ego stimulant, and we were seen together frequently.

"Two of my friends noticed, and worried about the direction this friendship was taking. They cared enough to talk to me directly about it.

"I was furious! How could they suspect anything? What kind of friends were these?

83

They were the ones with the dirty minds, not me. And I told them so.

"But inwardly the Holy Spirit convicted me immediately. We hadn't done anything wrong, but I was captivated by this woman, and the relationship was headed the wrong way.

"I argued with God, insisting that He was wrong. I swore that if it ever went further I'd break it off. I even spoke to the woman about it.

"Anyway, after a long period of very deep conviction, I abandoned that relationship which was headed for trouble. I began pouring my energies into my own marriage. As I did, I was astounded at the dry rot in my own marriage. It wasn't as secure as I'd thought.

"Anyway, to make a long story short, I am now finally able to look back over the past year with joy. Our life together has never been better. I see real growth in myself, my marriage, and our church.

"I just want to give credit to those two guys, who took such a big risk that day . . . if they hadn't offered that correction, who knows where that relationship might have led? I think I know. And I thank them for the correction."

Restoration is risky. But, where there is no risk, there is no gain. Likewise, where the risk is high, the gains are correspondingly high.

6. *Full restoration must come.* The whole purpose of restoration is to get the person back to where he was – and *often that even means leadership roles.* Why is it that the church will take an infamous sinner who has been saved out of the raw and propel him to leadership, while a fallen Christian forever forfeits any claim to leadership? It's a kind of Protestant penance, only worse – it never ends. Eventually a fallen Christian who clearly repents and reforms

should be restored completely, even to leadership. That doesn't mean such restoration should be immediate, and it doesn't mean that following a hasty repentance, the fallen Christian keeps all his responsibilities in the church as if nothing ever happened. On the contrary, a Christian who falls into obvious public sin should relinquish all leadership positions in the Church. But this should only be for a set time. He should be placed under a loving, spiritual mentor for accountability and growth. When a reasonable time has passed, he should be free to be appointed or elected to any post in the church. Restoration to fellowship is the fallen Christian's immediate need, not his restoration to leadership.

Now what about you, my friend?

Have you ever slipped off the straight and narrow path of obedience? Did Satan ever sneak up on your blind side and trip you up, sending you headlong into sin? Was there a time when you found yourself entangled in a habit, thought-pattern, or attitude which you couldn't seem to shake? Were you ever knocked over and swept away in an act of disobedience?

How did you want to be treated? With searing judgment and condemnation? Would you have been happy to have been simply ignored and "let be" to work it out yourself? Perhaps this is exactly what happened. Wouldn't it have been better if someone who loved you deeply had come to you with a tender and compassionate heart and carefully helped you back on track?

Did someone ever restore you? Certainly God has. We have all been restored by the gentle, strong arm of God. Most of us, many times. Now we who are restored, are to become restorers. Nice touch. We who have known disobedience ourselves now become God's instruments to restore other fellow travelers. It's the Christian way.

Bible Study

1. *Galatians 6:1-2.*

    — What is the descriptive word given to those equipped to be restorers?

    — In what ways should a restorer watch out for temptation himself?

    — How can a restorer "carry another's burden"?

2. *Luke 22:54-62.*

    — What sin did Peter commit in this incident?

    — How serious was Peter's sin? (see 1 John 2:23).

3. *John 21:15-17.* Reviewing Peter's restoration, observe what Jesus did and didn't do in restoring him:

    — Jesus DIDN'T . . .

— Jesus DID . . .

4. *1 John 5:16-17.*
   — Even if we don't get directly involved in restoring a fallen Christian, how are we supposed to pray?

   — What is the exception to this instruction to pray?

   — Many interpretations exist for the "sin that leads to death," in your opinion what could this mean?

5. *1 Corinthians 5:1-13.* What was the brother's sin in this case and what are the Christians told to do? Restore him? Why does Paul say this?

6. *2 Corinthians 2:5-8.*

   — What does Paul now tell the congregation to do regarding their infamous sinner?

- What do you think may have changed in the intervening time?

7. *1 Corinthians 4:21.*

    - What are the two general methods of discipline mentioned here?

    - Which method works best with you?

    - Which method are you generally more inclined toward personally?

    - Which do you think is the preferred method for restoring Christians?

8. *James 5:19-20.*

    - To whom is the writer talking . . . Christians?

    - What is it possible a brother may do?

    - What should someone else then do?

    - When this restoration is completed, what may the restorer have done?

9. Was I ever restored? If anyone ever offered correction or restoration to you, tell about it here. Did they do it wisely? Poorly? Did it work?

10. Where are our restorers? Those who are spiritual are the best equipped to do restoring. Who are the people in your local church who you think would be ideal restorers?

11. Is there someone I should restore? Using some sort of personal code or observations no one else would understand, list one or more persons for whom you might be a restorer.

12. Personal Reflection. What is one single thing you could do in response to the truths of this chapter?

— An action to take:

— A promise to make:

6
HUMILITY:
Putting off Pride

*Pride goes before destruction,
a haughty spirit
before a fall.*
　　　　　　　　　—Proverbs 16:18

Pride is a sinful attitude of superiority with a long-growing season. But sooner or later others sense your pride and come to dislike you for it. Eventually you see it yourself.

Pride sneaks up on a fellow. Several years ago I was traveling extensively on a speaking circuit. I would fly someplace almost every week and back. It was physically tiring but emotionally exhilarating. I enjoyed being used by the Lord in so many different cultures and among a variety of age groups.

91

As a souvenir of these trips I decided to keep the baggage tag hooked on the handle of my suitcase. On retrieving my suitcase after each trip I would tear off the tag and leave the string tied around the handle. Over the years an impressive cluster of strings built up until it looked like a massive carnation. I used it as a prayer reminder – to remember God's faithfulness in providing safe travel to me over the years.

But it also had an effect on others. Being younger than most speakers, I had always faced the attitude that I was a rookie who was getting a "good break to be invited here." Interestingly enough, as my baggage tags grew and bloomed, this attitude rapidly disappeared. Invariably the individual who picked me up would be impressed at how much I had traveled. I was impressed too, but hardly noticed it.

Then one day as I checked my bag for yet another flight, an enterprising counter clerk produced a knife and offered to "cut away these old strings." "I like them there . . . they're souvenirs" I protested. He shrugged his shoulders and checked the bag through to wherever I was going.

But as I walked to the gate, God's quiet voice spoke: "Why do you *really* want those baggage strings on your bag?" "Is it really for a prayer reminder or has it become something to impress others?" Throughout the entire flight I pondered His questions. Yes. I had to confess to pride. I had allowed Satan to take my simple collecting practice and twist it into evidence of a proud attitude. Before the flight ended that day I confessed to my pride and repented – turned away from the behavior. When I got to my room that day, I tore those strings off my suitcase one by one and dropped them into the wastebasket. Pride had quietly found a hiding place among my souvenir baggage tags . . . actually, in my heart.

Some might say I was too sensitive. But I knew

pride when I was confronted with it face to face. That's what's so funny about pride: we can sense it in others long before we see it in ourselves.

Do you have pride? Has this attitude sneaked in and curled up in some quiet corner of your heart? Putting off pride is a discipline we all must learn in order to walk obediently.

What is Pride?

Pride is thinking more highly of ourselves than we ought to think. It is an inaccurate overestimation of our accomplishments. Self-esteem, even self-love, is good for us. Pride, an overabundance of self-appreciation, is sin. It is a corruption of the essential self-love God expects us to have.

Pride may be the most deceitful of all sins, tucked deep within us, masked in a thousand ways. It has a treacherous influence on other attitudes.

The Bible speaks often about pride. Why? Because it is so common. This sin seems to be "natural." Some sins are more prevalent among certain age groups or in certain cultures. Pride knows no such bounds. It dwells among the young and old, rich and poor, east and west. If you visit a tiny backwoods village in Africa you will find pride. If you work in a gleaming tower in New York City, you'll find it there. Even among the poorest of folk, crammed into ghetto housing in steamy inner cities, pride finds a home. It is a common sin of mankind.

Not only is it common, it is widespread. Pride runs both wide and deep. It mingles with a multitude of other vices forming a poisonous brew. Pride tends to bond with other vices.

Worse than blending with our vices, pride fuses with our virtues. The further along you are in your spiritual walk, the more likely you are to encounter the monster of pride. When you have overcome outward sins, even found victory over sinful inner attitudes and thoughts, Satan unleashes this secret weapon. No longer can he easily drag you away into outward sin. Perhaps now Satan is often beaten when attempting to entice you into inner sins like wrong thoughts and attitudes. So, he begins to flatter you. Satan reminds you how spiritually minded you are . . . how far you've come . . . how much farther along you are than many – perhaps most – others. You begin believing it. Soon devilish spiritual pride mates with your spirit and produces a litter of other sins. Pride tends to mix with both vices and virtues.

"Acceptable Pride"

We are not talking here about justifiable pride – the sensible appreciation of fine work of craftsmanship. An obedient Christian might take pride in his city, new church, neat lawn, or children (more so, grandchildren). These are usually reasonable levels of gratification in how things are turning out. If you are going to buy a handmade cabinet or chest you will want a carpenter who "takes pride in his work." This kind of dignity in a job well done is expected of a "workman worthy of his hire."

Just as there is such a thing as righteous anger, so there is righteous pride . . . a sense of legitimate satisfaction. The Apostle Paul was proud of the Corinthian Church's response after his first letter to them, and he said so.

However, like righteous anger, justifiable pride is a slippery slope. Our human spirit tends to justify sin. I sat in a Sunday school class in Pennsylvania where they were discussing how to tell the difference between justifiable pride and sinful pride. One fellow concluded the discussion with, "That's easy: *your* pride is sin; *mine's* justifiable." His comment was greeted with laughter, then the teacher moved on to the next verse.

It is too often true. We can easily rationalize our own pride while condemning our brother's or sister's. So, while we can accept a certain level of self-respect, dignity in work, and satisfaction in others, we must always be aware that even this "healthy pride" can turn sour, self-serving and sinful.

What Causes Pride?

Pride is so universal it seems not to be the result of cause and effect. It appears to be stamped on the essential nature of humanity. However, there are some conditions which enhance the "breeding environment" so that pride is more easily cultured. These factors tend to cultivate pride. If one or more are descriptive of your life, you may need to be on your guard against this sin.

1. Success. Once we've achieved success we tend to take credit for it. Others encourage us to do this. Once you've "made it" everyone assumes you know the "secret of success." You are showered with admiration, applause, and invitations to share the secrets which made you successful. Others hungering to succeed listen intently, take notes, and supply generous amounts of flattery. You've made it . . . after all, you *must* be smarter than everybody else, right? The more successful you are, the greater your temptation to pride. You eventually may come to believe all the praise. Are you successful? If so, beware of pride.

2. Knowledge. If pride lives in your heart, the more you know, the more stupid everyone else will appear to be. Being an expert in your field can make it difficult to put up with the "idiots the schools are producing nowadays." It's easy to forget that everything you know, you once had to learn. Intellectual arrogance shows no pity on the unlearned. It is impatient with common people.

That is not to say that you should avoid learning

(any more than you should avoid success). Success and the ability to learn are gifts of God to be accepted with gratitude. However, as with all gifts, they can also become curses. The dark side of knowledge is the tendency to pride. "Knowledge puffs up." And, "A little knowledge puffs up even more." The most dangerous fool of all is the college sophomore who became a "know-it-all" in two quick years of college. Those who truly pursue knowledge eventually discover how little they know.

Are you knowledgeable? Watch out for pride!

3. Wealth. Many proud people are not wealthy. Few wealthy folk are not proud. The prestige, power, influence, position, and possessions of the rich naturally promote pride. Fine clothing, expensive automobiles, and the exquisitely decorated homes of the rich all join together in harmony to laud the importance of the one commanding it all. He is likely to believe it.

In the church we love rich people. We scurry to please them, place them on boards and committees quickly after they are saved, and listen intently if they are unhappy with anything. We flatter, cajole, and charm them. We shower the rich with compliments and salute their handsome gifts to the church. It's as if we had returned to the Middle Ages. In this we sin. Not only do we break the commandments of James 2, but we lay a great snare about the feet of the wealthy.

We wouldn't think of lavishing a converted drunkard with gifts of 100-proof whiskey. We know of his tendency to drink and would avoid tempting him. Then why do we lay such a trap for the rich and powerful? Are we trying to trip this brother and send him skidding into his besetting sin?

Are you wealthy? Then watch out for pride. Pride is an occupational hazard of wealth.

4. Creativity. What a gift from God, yet a tool

of Satan! An irony: the more talented and creative you are, the more likely you are to see how things "ought to be done." There are some people who could do just about any job they wanted – at church or work – and they could do it better than most anyone else. They simply know how to do things well – everything. Perhaps you are one of those persons.

The danger of creativity is arrogance. Assuming that everybody else is a moron, you offer to everybody your answers to all problems. You've got the solution for your work, your church, your denomination, the country. People nod and listen, seldom arguing with you – for you probably *are* right. But they resent you for it. You are marked as a cocky know-it-all. Your spirit oozes conceit. Unless talent and creativity are harnessed and directed into proper channels you will wind up on the sidelines of life, evaluating everything from your own superior perspective. You may be right. But eventually you'll have no one to tell. All will avoid you like the plague. You have become arrogant. If you are extremely talented and creative, beware of pride.

5. Talent. The better you are at something the greater the danger of pride. In what areas do you have talent? Is your talent natural or acquired? Is it music? Is it art? athletics? academics? leading? Is there some area where you seem to have natural talent? If so, the tendency is to elevate yourself, as if you are somehow better than others, and this talent is the evidence of it. The performance talents – those which are oriented toward entertaining crowds – are especially prone to be breeding grounds for pride.

Are you talented? Beware of pride.

6. Virtue. What? Virtue? In what way could goodness be a breeding ground of pride? Irony of ironies: the better you are, the filthier your temptations. For when you have achieved spiritual success, you may become a target of the most contemptible pride of all – spiritual pride. With spiritual achievement, pride slithers in. You are tempted to pour contempt on all others who have not come as far as you. You seem *so* spiritual. And these others, these carnal Christians . . . why, they are so shallow and simple. If only they could grow up like me . . ." And you become guilty of a worse sin than they. If you are a mature, adult Christian, far beyond the "babe in Christ" you once were, thank God for the virtue He has created in you, but beware of the devil's newest trap: pride.

The Trouble with Pride

Whatever the cause, pride's results are devastating. The seed of pride inevitably produces a bad crop. Exposing its final destination may urge us to turn around before it's too late. Here's the trouble with pride:

1. God hates pride. God hates pride perhaps more than any other sin. He has resolved to expose and punish it. Pride makes Him angry. He has promised in His Word to bring low those who elevate themselves. And He will keep His word. If you are intent on pleasing God, you must be cleansed of pride, for He will not abide it. This alone should be enough reason to abandon all pride, present and future.

2. Men will hate us. People love to watch the fall of a great man. "The bigger they are, the harder they fall," we gleefully say. Most folk secretly revel in the demise of a great, proud man or woman. But this is not the worst of it. It's waiting for the fall . . . the yearning for another's collapse which is the greater evil. Pride provides the temptation of others to envy – that unseemly desire to see the downfall of another. The more pride others see in you, the more they will hope for *your* downfall. Proud people may have power, prestige, money, and influence. But the proud have few friends.

3. Pride ignites other sins. It is difficult to commit one sin. Sin comes in clusters. Pride is especially prone to blend with other sins. At the very least pride will lead to boasting – "being proud out loud." After all, once you are convinced of your greatness, why not tell others? But pride also leads to arrogance, conceit, vanity, and haughtiness. You will eventually become cocky and condescending, totally wrapped up in yourself. If pride is not eliminated early, it can eventually make a hated, egotistical person out of you.

4. You will undervalue others. He who overestimates himself undervalues others. The higher and better you think you are, the lower and lesser you will assume everyone else is. Pride leads you to disdain others. Inevitably you will come to dismiss both the person's work and the person himself as insignificant. If you have the power, your scorn for others will result in your creating an oppressive atmosphere where you rule as absolute monarch – at work, school, and worst of all, at home. Eventually you will dismiss others – even loved ones – as idiots, morons, or stooges, wondering to yourself, "Why do I have to do *everything* around here . . . can't someone else do things right just once?"

5. Pride produces resentment in others. If you are a proud boss, you'll produce resentment in your employees. If you are not the boss, your pride produces resentment inside yourself. You'll say, "I deserve to be treated better than this. All they're doing is using me. I get no recognition around here." "I'm really the key to this place; without me, everything would fall apart." If you are proud, but not on top, watch out for resentment and bitterness. Either way, whether you are the boss or worker, pride produces resentment – in others or yourself.

6. *Attempts to impress others.* No proud person will be satisfied in being his only admirer. Pride drives us to all sorts of attempts to make others think we're great. The proud person will attempt to impress others with indulgent and excessive living. The proud man will try name-dropping to show how important he is. The proud woman delights in telling "power-stories" of how she wielded her influence or wealth. The proud person does not recognize how others see through these pitiful attempts to inflate personal greatness. He or she thinks their practice of name-dropping and their expensive life-style has actually impressed everybody. But the people are not fooled. How pitiful, the life of the proud.

7. *Pride makes us "practical atheists."* Perhaps this is why God reserves special wrath for pride. In pride, we discard gratitude to God and assume that we ourselves have accomplished our success. We become our own creators and sustainers of life – becoming guilty of the master sin: self-worship. Who needs God? We can do it ourselves! We've *already* done it ourself. Is atheism far behind? Is this not what C. S. Lewis calls "practical atheism?" No wonder God urges us to put off pride!

Pride usurps the glory rightfully due God and others. Why do you have wealth? Success? Knowledge? Talent? Creativity? Virtue? Did you get it yourself? Do you think you really are a self-made man or woman? Do you worship your "creator?" Or do you have others to thank? Isn't it true that you have nothing but what came to you by the hand of God and others? Pride will tell you otherwise. Pride lies – and then it utterly destroys.

8. *Pride eventually leads to collapse.* Pride leads

to overconfidence. The more we inflate our self-opinion, the more we become cocky, rash, and confident that *we* are "the exception." We are above the laws of God and man – or so we act. The more successful we become, the more we risk. Finally our unrealistic life breaks with reality. Life comes crashing down around our ears. We've overextended our sensible limits. This is God's natural law. God has spoken: "Pride goes before destruction, a haughty spirit before a fall," (Prov. 16:18). There is no such thing as permanent pride. It is bound to collapse.

As a child, I remember my dad telling me the ancient fable of the eagle and the frog:

> One day an eagle glided down to the edge of a mud puddle to quench his thirst. Nearby was a frog who had been watching enviously as the eagle had circled lazily in the sky. The frog hatched a brilliant idea.
>
> "How about taking me up for a ride?" the frog proposed, "I've invented a way." The frog continued, "You simply grab the end of this stick in your beak, and I'll bite on to my end as you fly."
>
> The eagle agreed. Exerting all the strength he could muster, the eagle took off into the sky with the frog trailing along with the other end of the stick firmly in his mouth. The frog was absolutely dazzled by the sights from the sky. His invention was a monumental success.
>
> Soon hundreds of other birds gathered around to praise this new idea. The flock included starlings, bluejays, robins, crows, and many others. "Amazing!" "Fantastic!" "Marvelous," they said. "With this new idea, thousands of frogs will be able to see the great sights of the sky." They cheered the resourcefulness of the new concept. Then one large crow, obviously their spokesman, asked, "Who thought of this great invention?" The frog, swelling with

pride, answered, "I . . ." (Splaat)!

So it is with pride. Just when we open our mouths to take credit for our success, we lose our grip on life and plunge back to earth – to the mud puddle where it all began. Pride leads to collapse and spiritual death.

Putting off Pride

We have met this monster pride, and have come to recognize its causes and consequences. But, how to get rid of it? Do *you* have pride? Does this all sound familiar or strange to you?

If you are moving along in your Christian walk, growing in maturity, take some time for self-examination on this point. During times of such quiet thought we often hear God's quiet voice gently pointing out a sprout of pride. A day alone with God or a morning quiet time may give God the opportunity to speak. Most of us are so busy that a tiny sprout of pride can grow to become a full vine, entwining about all our attitudes before we notice. Give God a chance. Take some time to listen. He is faithful, and will convict your heart if this is an area for which you should seek His cleansing. Pray, "Search me, O God . . ." If He convicts you of pride, take the prescriptions offered here:

1. Confess and repent. Start by openly admitting your sinful pride before the Lord. Then make a decision to turn away from it with full intention to never turn back. This is confession and repentance. There will be no healing until you first admit your need.

2. Spend time with "humblers." Some people are marvelously gifted at humbling others. I'm not talking about negative-thinking balloon-poppers who delight in putting people down with caustic and sarcastic taunts. Rather, I mean certain people who are clever, fast-thinking, and witty – people who don't take others too seriously. Being with people like this can help you to quit taking yourself so seriously. I've known whole groups like this who meet for coffee break every day. Few who attend such gatherings will be troubled with pride very long. It just won't last in such an atmosphere.

If you know such a person or group, spend some time with them on purpose. It is hard to be proud around these folk. Their remarks will remind you of who you really are. Children are especially good "humblers." Adults don't awe them. They simply know you as Dad, Mom, or Grandpa. Like the little boy who announced that the emperor had no clothes on, they see us for what we really are. If you have no associates who humble you periodically, find some. Take this medicine; it will be good for you.

3. Occasionally compare yourself upwards. Generally, comparison does little good at all. But the proud man or woman has gotten into the habit of comparison – downward. He surveys those scattered below him comparing them to his own great achievements. These underachievers seem so puny from his perspective. He thus sustains his grandiose view of himself. The prescription: simply reverse this habit. Compare yourself *upward.* Are you a superb golfer? Watch the Masters Tournament. Are you wealthy? Compare yourself with some of the *really* wealthy people. Do you think you are the best preacher in your area? Sit under the feeding ministry of a great old "war horse" preacher and watch your "preacher-pride" wither.

I once sat on a board which was deciding if they wanted to move their offices from a small town to a major city. One fellow argued for staying in the small town. He said, "If we move to a big city, nobody will even notice us, but here in this town we can be a big fish in a little pond."

Sometimes our own importance is inflated merely because we've been swimming in little ponds. There is always someone, somewhere who is far richer, smarter, faster, better; or more successful, creative, and virtuous than we are. When we get into a large enough pond, we are soon humbled. Are you proud? Compare yourself upwards a bit.

4. Adopt humbling disciplines. If you battle with pride, purposely adopt several disciplines of humility. Return some grocery carts to the store from the parking lot. Stop on your way to the office and spend ten minutes picking up paper on the lawn. Change a tire on someone's car. Pick up paper scraps and straighten out the hymnals after service one day. Are these chores beneath you? Try to think of several humbling disciplines you could start to continually deflate your pride. Jesus washed His disciples' feet as such a discipline. What could *you* do?

5. Seek cleansing. Perhaps "putting off pride" is a deceiving subtitle for this section. Pride is not something outward we can easily drop aside. There are such things in the Bible. We are simply told to put them off, like old clothing or clinging burrs picked up after a walk in the woods. Pride is different. It resides within. Deep within. "Put off" may be an inadequate concept for getting rid of pride. Two other biblical terms may better describe the need: "cleansing" and "crucifixion."

Anyone who has wrestled with pride knows it is not easily dropped aside like a dirty piece of clothing. It clings to our nature, forming an alloy with the metal of our soul. We who fight it need something radical. We need *cleansing* – a God-initiated purifying act in our hearts. We seek *crucifixion* – the execution of this evil inclination within. Certainly we must do our part. But only God can complete the work of purification necessary to cleanse us of pride. And He is faithful. He will do it. God catalogs no sin from which His followers cannot be free. God's grace is greater than all our sin. Even a taint so deep as pride!

Now, what about you, my friend?

Do you have pride? These are heavy thoughts, aren't they? Exposing pride has not been an easy task. It's neither fun nor entertaining to read. But pride is a troublesome sin which God would like to remove from your life. And He will do it. Do you have pride? *Any* pride? If so, confess it to our Lord. Seek His forgiveness and cleansing. You can trust Him. After all, cleansing is His business.

Of course you should be careful not to become obsessed with this sin which must be expelled from your life. Sometimes we assume if all our sins were cast out of our hearts we would be a perfect Christian. Wrong. Each of these homeless devils would gather seven other devils and return to again occupy the empty houses of our souls. We would be worse off than before. Nature abhors a vacuum; so does God. Perfection is not emptiness.

Rather, you must fill your mind and soul with good things (Phil. 4:8). Virtues are much stronger than vices. For every vice there is an unequal and opposite virtue. For pride, it's humility. Do you hunger for a meek and humble spirit which makes a completely accurate estimate of yourself – neither inflated nor depressed? Do you yearn for the humility that prompts service? Do you always look for opportunities to affirm other people, forever seeking to encourage, praise, and honor others? Do you crave this kind of attitude . . . the humble attitude which Jesus had?

You can have it. All this and more are included in God's plan for your life. Humility. What a beautiful trait. Is this what you want? Are you thirsty enough to drink in great gulps of Christ's humility?

God resists the proud, but He gives grace to the humble. Ask God for an avalanche of humility in your life. He can cleanse your pride and fill you with a humble spirit.

Try Him and see!

Bible and Life

1. Proverbs 8:13. What is God's attitude toward "pride" and its traveling companion, "arrogance"?

2. Proverbs 13:10. According to this verse, pride is the breeding ground for what? Why do you think this is so?

3. 2 Kings 5:11. About whom is this verse speaking? What does this verse tell you about him?

4. Daniel 4:28-30. What statement should Nebuchadnezzar have made?

5. *Philippians 2:3-11.*

— How are we commanded to consider others in relation to ourselves (v. 3)?

— What is included in "looking to our own interests" (v. 4)?

— In what ways was Christ an example of humility?

6. *1 Peter 5:6.* If we intentionally humble ourselves, what does God promise to do?

7. *2 Corinthians 7:4; 8:24.* What level or types of pride would be acceptable to God?

8. *Galatians 6:4.* What secret is given here which can help us avoid both extremes: the inflated ego and low self-image?

9. *Personal reflection.* Of what can I be legitimately "proud"?

10. *Personal reflection.* If pride were to become a personal problem for me, at what point might Satan attempt to breed pride in me?

11. *Personal reflection.* What is one thing you could and should do in response to the truths you have discovered in this study?

— An action to take:

— A promise to make:

7
AMBITIONS:
Abandoning Selfish Ambition

Whoever wants to become great among you must be your servant.
                              Matthew 20:26

Do *you want to be great?* Do you have a burning passion to leave your tracks on the sand of history? Do you hunger for success? Do you desperately want to "make it" in life? Would people call you a "go-getter" or "ambitious"? Are you "on your way to the top"? If these sorts of words describe your quest for success, perhaps you have sometimes wondered if your healthy dose of ambition has tinges of selfishness in it.

Several years ago a bright young fellow on his

way to success posed a serious question. This guy was a hard-working, promising lad. He always showed up, did his assignments with excellence, and inevitably put out the extra effort to achieve excellence. I call this sort of fellow a "sharpy," "producer" or "comer."

This bright young man came to me deeply disturbed. He wondered if his motivation was wholly proper. He thought there must be such a thing as good ambition. But he wasn't sure his unquenchable thirst for success was pure. In fact, he confessed he suspected it was mostly impure. He sensed he wanted to get ahead simply for the power, prestige, money, and influence it would bring him. "Is this wrong?" was his question.

What would you have said? What's the difference between good ambition and carnal one-upmanship? How can you tell which you have?

There are some people who worry too much about their motivations. These Christians don't get much done in the world because they're always checking themselves for improper motivations. Like hypochondriacs, they constantly invent spiritual illnesses. This is the devil's trick to keep such tender Christians preoccupied with themselves instead of a needy world. I'm not addressing these remarks to such folk. If you have such an extraordinary sensitivity, this might even be a chapter to skip.

However, if you seldom worry about your motivations, and are a hard-driving, success-oriented person, the Lord may have some words specifically for you in this chapter.

Motivation and Ambition

Right intentions can purify a foul deed. The New Testament repeatedly reminds us that we can be judged "blameless" by God if our intention is pure . . . even though the actual result falls pitifully below the absolute standard of perfection. Because of ignorance or spiritual immaturity, we may offer up a "spotted sacrifice" to God in our words, thoughts, or deeds. Yet, if our intention was pure – completely hungry to please God – He pronounces us "blameless" in His sight. God holds us accountable for what we say, think, or do *purposefully.*

In this, God does nothing more than we would do. For instance, last year my house was in desperate need of painting. Due to a pressing travel and speaking schedule, I determined to hire a painter to do the job. After mentioning it one night at the dinner table, my twelve-year-old son piped up, "Hey, Dad, I'll paint the house . . . I really could use the money." What was I to do? I took the risk and gave him the job.

He recruited another twelve-year-old to help him and plunged into the work with a hearty vigor (which began to wane during the hot days of August)! After several weeks he had finished the job and was ready for my final inspection and his payday. He had worked harder than I had ever seen him work before. I could see that he had taken special care to avoid spilling drops of paint and splotching the trim paint on the siding. He had carefully scraped and peeled away large slabs of the old paint before adding the fresh coat. In some places he had carefully applied two coats to ensure complete coverage.

As we slowly examined our way around the house, I noticed an occasional slip-up – a smudge of blue trim on the siding, or a few drops of yellow paint on the shrubs. As we completed the final inspection I was remembering that he had never painted anything before in his life. I was justifiably proud of his hard work. As we finished the tour, he turned and gazed expectantly into my face. "How'd I do, Dad?" he asked.

What do you think I said? I responded, "David, you've done a *perfect* job!" and gave him a great bear hug in appreciation. I paid him . . . even gave him a bonus.

Would God do less? No. He considers our experience, the difficulty of our assignment, our maturity, and the motivations of our heart. Like a loving father, He sometimes pronounces our work "perfect" even when *He* can see a smudge here and there. Only God has the wisdom to pronounce us blameless. Only He knows our true motivations. When our motivation is pure, God pronounces our deed pure.

Conversely, a pure deed can be polluted by foul motivations. Jesus reserved His most scathing condemnation for the Pharisees. They loved to engage in holy activities – especially praying and giving – but did these things out of impure motivation . . . to be seen of men or considered holy. An impure motivation can defile the best of deeds.

So what does all of this have to do with ambition? Much! Ambition in itself is not wrong. Sin enters the picture at the motivation level. *Why* are we ambitious? It is our motivation for getting ahead and the methods we use which determines the sinfulness of ambition. Consider three levels of ambition:

1. *Holy Ambition*

Some ambition is outright "holy." Holy ambition is a pure, pointed mandate from God. It is a call to complete a task or a mission. It is closely connected with the ideas of "call" or "destiny." Holy ambition is knowing for sure that God is calling you to do something. You believe you have "come to the kingdom for just such a time as this." It is hungering for obedience to your Master more than for mere accomplishment and success. Holy ambition produces a calm, unruffled drive like that of Jesus Christ, who never seemed to be in a hurry yet always knew where He was headed. Holy ambition is the conviction that God has called you to do something, and nothing in or under the world can stop you. It is a holy compulsion driving you to achievement as a matter of obedience, not as a matter of personal success.

Holy ambition drives you to succeed because you believe this is God's will for you. Not a general kind of will – in the sense that God expects all of us to do a good job – but in a personal way. It is a compulsion from God. You feel that God has "called" you personally to achieve this thing. You believe that God intends to accomplish this special work through you. It is *His* will, not yours. You are certain that this is God's will for your life, and you feel "destined" to achieve it.

Holy ambition isn't common.

2. Human Aspiration

This kind of ambition is neither good nor bad, it is simply human. God has created us with a longing for achievement, fulfillment, even greatness. We have a hunger for significance, a desire for something better, something lasting. All of us have this yearning, Christian or not. This innate desire to achieve, to create, to improve, is stamped on our nature by the Creator. It is a glimpse of one way we are "created in His image." It is a drive to do better, to accomplish something, to leave something worthwhile behind us.

These human aspirations are not sin, they are wholesome. This desire for excellence, accomplishment, and betterment comes from God. Most all progress in civilization springs from this God-given drive. Christians, of all people, should fan these human embers of achievement into flame, for He is "able to do immeasurably more than all we ask or *imagine,* according to his power that is at work within us" (Eph. 3:20 NIV). Most of us are achieving far below our potential. If we fear success, somehow thinking that failure is holy or honorable, we are wrong. Jesus clearly taught that the man who buries his potential in the ground will receive strict rejection from his Master (Matt. 25:26).

God expects you to invest and multiply the talents and opportunities He has given you. For He is the one who has given you the desires of human aspiration. These are neither good nor bad – what they *lead* to will determine their goodness or badness.

3. Selfish Ambition

Here is the lowest level of ambition. Selfish ambition crosses the line from human aspiration into selfishness because the motivation is impure. Selfish ambition is sin. It springs from the flesh. It is the desire to be lord over others – to possess the power of success. It is the desire to beat others, be number one, win for winning's sake. It is "healthy competition" turned into "hellish combativeness." Selfish ambition is a hunger for power, prestige, and status. It thirsts for recognition, rewards, and the influence which comes with success. This kind of ambition propels men and women to trample competitors under foot and to climb over friends to achieve success. Once a person with selfish ambition makes it to the next highest level, he or she quickly kicks down old friends who helped him or her get there. They are no longer useful in climbing to the next step of greatness. It is this third variety of ambition which is sin and out of place in the Christian's life.

Mixed Motivation

For most of us, our aspirations cannot be neatly divided between the three levels: sometimes there is *mixed motivation* in our desire for achievement. While we may not claim that our ambition is of the holy type, we usually feel it is of the wholesome, human variety. At least, mostly so. *Mostly?* Herein lies the problem of selfish ambition. Who would say that their ambition is *wholly* selfish? Few. Such a person is not a Christian at all. But a believer may come to recognize that his ambition is *partly* selfish.

Satan does not attempt to turn wholesome ambition into evil in a day or even a year. Rather, he injects the poison of selfish ambition . . . one drop at a time. Each tiny additional drop seems minute compared with the whole. We may not even recognize this poisoning process at first. Even when we recognize it, we dismiss this *part* of our motivation as inconsequential. Then we comfort ourselves with the thought that our motivation is "mostly" pure.

But these tiny drops of selfish ambition multiply and taint our entire motivation. The devil, once given a foothold, is intent on expanding his territory. Like yeast, selfish ambition soon spreads its influence throughout the whole dough of our heart.

No serious Christian can be satisfied with ambition which is "mostly pure." That part of our ambition which is selfish must be cleansed, or it will stain the whole.

Degenerating Ambition

Ambition has a tendency to start out right, then get off track. Human aspiration can be 100% wholesome at first, yet later derail into selfish ambition. We can start out with a clean God-given desire to succeed; yet, as time passes, selfish ambition leaks into our motivation and we become selfish. We must constantly be on guard against the devil's attempts to introduce microscopic molecules of selfish ambition into our motivation. We must be constantly aware of these attempts to subvert our wholesome human motivation. It is clear that human aspiration can degenerate into selfish ambition.

Being "Power Hungry"

Even more serious is the degeneration of holy ambition into selfish ambition. God may call a man or woman to some great task. At first, this person's motivation is completely holy. He or she is obsessed with following God and God alone. However, as this great man or woman finds success, Satan begins to introduce the twin sisters of success: pride and selfish ambition. Soon our spiritual giant allows selfish ambition to make its bed beside the original holy ambition. The two lie together, and the "great man of God" becomes tainted by selfish ambition.

This is the danger of seeking a powerful anointing from God.

Do you hunger for more power from God? Have you heard stories of D. L. Moody and Charles Finney who merely strolled through factories and people fell under a powerful spell of conviction . . . just being in their presence? Do you yearn for this kind of anointing? If so, God may answer your prayer. Seeking is the way to finding.

Many pray for this power from God. In fact, there is an increasing number every year. Their desire seems so pure, so consecrated . . . so godly. Yet, underneath it all there is often something dark going on. Their desire for power from God is sometimes impure. They crave God's power for selfish purposes. They yearn for the success and fame which accompany God's anointing. They covet the *benefits* of God's anointing more than the anointing itself.

Sometimes God answers these selfish prayers. Startling, isn't it? He sometimes grants power to unworthy vessels. I know of one preacher who led a great moving of the Spirit in a meeting . . . yet several afternoons that week, he sneaked off to a nearby adult bookstore to feed his own lustful cravings. Another powerful preacher was having great outpourings of God in his camp meetings, yet for years he had been lying about his past achievements, even inventing a fictitious doctorate for himself. A great author who had a powerful influence on my life turned out to be an adulterer.

What's going on here? How can men or women have such power when they are hollow inside? Once the truth comes out, we ascribe their use by God to mere human charisma or crowd psychology. We are wrong. They probably were anointed. God does not always immediately withdraw His power or authority from corrupt vessels. Frightening, isn't it?

How could God do such a thing as this? Why does He not reserve His power for only the purest and most deserving of His followers? Why grant it to hollow men or women? We don't like the answer: He sometimes imparts His power to such men and women so that all will eventually see their true inner bankruptcy.

For outward power and inward purity are two different things. Men who seek God's outward power, yet do not have His inward purity, are destined to eventual collapse. Their great ministries are "houses of cards" – the higher they go, the greater their fall. When God answers their prayer for power, they are increasingly used in the Kingdom. They plunge onward and upward, constructing an ever-expanding ministry teetering on a foundation of sand. Finally, their personal tower of Babel reaches God's predetermined limit. It all comes crashing down in moral collapse. They exit in ridicule and humiliation.

The rest of us scurry about covering up the mess to preserve God's reputation and the church's good name. It doesn't work. The truth gets out. Everyone eventually discovers that this "great leader" was a hollow hero. His outer shell was magnificent, but his inner moral timber was infested with termites.

Yet God is glorified. How? Following his downfall, the church lays aside its secular preoccupation with outward power and talks in hushed tones about the importance of inward purity for a time.

Do you hunger for more power from God? Have you been selfishly seeking God's outer anointing on your life? Beware. Just as He answered Israel's prayer for a king, God may answer your prayer. But if you do not have His inner purity, you too will collapse.

It is clear, isn't it? Even our quest in spiritual matters may become tainted with selfish ambition. Like Simon Magus, we can hunger for God's power with selfish motivation (Acts 8:19-21).

How to Recognize Selfish Ambition

But how are we to know if our ambition is selfish? Is there some test we can take? Is there some wise sage we can visit who can tell us for sure? It's not that easy. However, with some reflection, the Holy Spirit is always reliable to point out sin in our lives. This is His work. Give Him a chance to speak, and you can be sure that if you have any selfish ambitions, He will expose it. Ponder the following questions as you listen to the Spirit. Is He saying anything to you? With Samuel, tell Him, "Speak, Lord, your servant listens." If He points out something, respond obediently. If you hear nothing, then joyfully move on to the next chapter with a clear heart. But if He speaks, seek His cleansing of your ambitions. Ponder these questions. Perhaps grade yourself with an A, B, C, D in each of the areas:

1. Am I more interested in the glory than the goal?

2. How do I feel when someone else starts to accomplish "my thing," or fulfills my dream . . . do I rejoice or have a tinge of jealousy or envy?

3. Am I preoccupied with the means more than the goal?

4. Do I visualize *myself* doing or being the dream, or do I visualize the recipients receiving the benefit of my work? Is it need-

oriented or ego-oriented?

5. Am I infatuated with power, money, prestige, influence?

6. Is my ambition short-term, or has it been long lasting in my life? Has it "marinated" for several years, or is it really merely a temporary brainstorm?

7. Is it specific and definable, or inspecific and hard to explain?

8. Is it need-oriented – growing out of a burden to serve people, or does it grow out of *my* desire for achievement?

9. Do leaders – those in spiritual and administrative authority over me – give me confirmation of this ambition? Do they say, "Go for it," or are they giving caution signals?

10. Do those around me "sign up," volunteering to help me accomplish this great ambition?

11. Am I obsessed with the accomplishment of this great goal?

12. Am I willing to "pay the price" to see it happen, or do I want someone to hand it to me on a silver platter?

13. Can I see it . . . can I visualize the results?

14. Do my spouse, parents, and other Christians confirm this ambition to me?

15. Would I feel "released" if God raised up somebody else who did it better than I?

16. Have I dropped past friends and associates who helped get me where I am?

17. In what way would God get glory if I achieved my deepest ambition?

18. Have I compromised any of my personal standards to get where I now am?

Prescription for Selfish Ambition

Do you sense that part of your ambition is stained with selfishness? What are you to do? Is there a means of purifying your human ambition? How will you keep it pure?

This is not one of those areas where you seek a single cleansing, then forget the problem forevermore. True, you may need a crisis cleansing of your selfish ambition. You may need to "die out to your dreams." You may need to offer up your dreams on the altar. But dead ambition may rise again to haunt you. The devil doesn't give up that easily.

However, you need not feel that you are plagued with this sin forevermore. Selfish ambition can be crucified. If you take the antidote, the poison of selfish ambition can be neutralized in your soul.

1. Reflection. Take some time for introspection. Not the morbid kind of self-abuse some do, but a positive time of silence and listening before the Lord. Give Him a chance to speak. He is not an angry, brutish God seeking to crush you under the load of your weaknesses and sin. Rather, He is a loving Shepherd seeking to gently nudge you onto the paths of righteousness. Take some time – at least a bit – for Him to nudge you. Don't put this book down without taking a few minutes to listen to what He has to say to you. Read over the list of questions listed earlier. Ask, "Is my ambition selfish? Any *part* of it?"

2. Call it by name. If you sense the Lord pointing out selfishness in your desire to achieve, call it by name: selfish ambition . . . sin. Until we concede a particular attitude is sin, we will seldom see it purified. Once we call it by name, victory and cleansing can come. Be honest. Name it.

3. Confess to another. It may not be absolutely necessary, but you will make great strides toward victory if you share your inclination to selfish ambition with a dear friend. This humbling act will give you a powerful jump start toward banishing selfish impurity from your ambition. This person may even agree to hold you accountable . . . checking in with you from time to time on the extent of your progress in casting out selfish ambition. If you were to do this, with whom could you share such a thing? Is there someone you could trust enough to confess this selfishness to him or her?

4. Die out. It's an old-fashioned term, but worthy of reconsideration today. Die out! It means surrendering personal hopes, aspirations, and dreams on God's altar of commitment. It is sacrificing your personal ambitions on the altar of consecration, like Abraham offered up his son. Dying out is surrendering your most precious desires for achievement to the Lord, assuming you will never get it back. (You may, but if you assume so the sacrifice is not totally surrendered.)

Dying sometimes takes time. Though there is such a thing as "sudden death," more often death is a slow (and painful) process. You may enter a *period* of dying out. Selfish ambition dies slowly. It tenaciously clings to life. This sin may die at once, or die gradually, but you can start the process of execution.

5. Recognize that God's focus is inward. Our secular mindset sometimes overtakes us. We assume

God, like us, is more concerned with what He does *through* us than what He does *in* us. In this we err. If God has a preoccupation, it is with our inside – our attitudes, thoughts, motivations, and personal purity. Inside quality lasts; outside quantity fades. When we realize God is more concerned with our inner attitudes than our outward success, we will be able to lay aside our secular fixation with "climbing the ladder."

6. Focus on Christ as your example. Are you ambitious? Then think of Christ. How would you measure *His* success? Was Jesus a "winner"? Would you consider Jesus Christ a high achiever? Was He a ladder climber? How high did *He* climb? Did He make it to the top?

He did! The height of His career was played out at the top of Calvary's hill. Like us, His disciples wondered who would have the place of precedence – to His right and left – when He came into His kingdom (Matthew 20:21). When Jesus hung on Calvary's hill to the right and left hung unknown thieves, on cruel crosses.

Jesus "had it all." He was God's Son. He was *God.* "Very God" reads most creeds. Yet *He* humbled himself to become a man, a common carpenter. He chose to be obedient to God. This was success for Him. Obedience. Even unto death. Painful death. Death on a cross.

And what did the Father do? God then exalted Him to the highest place of all. Didn't the Father give *Him* a name which will ultimately send every knee bowing? Isn't this how the Father responds to humble servanthood?

In our obsession with our own success we sometimes lose sight of Jesus Christ. We "pig out" on "success formula talks" by others who have "made it." Each has his or her own "ten steps to success" for us. Some flaunt their wealth, influence, and power as evidence of their success. We are impressed. We too begin to hunger for worldly wealth, fame, power. And selfish ambition is born.

Rather, we should look to Jesus. We should seek the attitude Jesus had: willingness to "give it all up" in order to obey the Father. Jesus' example inspires true success: *obedience.*

7. *Seek cleansing.* Some sins we can lay aside with God's help. Others we can seemingly drop ourselves. A few sins, however, require radical surgery from God. Selfish ambition will not be beaten by a simple 1-2-3 "how to overcome" prescription. God's grace is great enough to forgive you of this sin. But His grace is even greater than that: He will cleanse you of this inclination. God's grace is radical! It seeks nothing less than the total transformation of your entire life into Christlikeness. If you have selfish ambition, you must do something about it. But you need not rid yourself of this taint by yourself. God is able to grant you transforming power to correct this fleshly attitude. His grace is great enough to cleanse this selfishness of the spirit, purifying your ambition. This is the kind of God you serve!

Now, what about you, my friend?

Has God pricked your own soul about your ambition? Do not listen to the voices about you. Listen to God alone. What does *He* say? Do you have selfish ambition? Is your ambition *partly* selfish? If so, seek God's cleansing. Seek the death of this yeast before it spreads its evil leaven into the whole loaf of life. God will do it. He is in the transforming business. Ask Him and see!

Bible Study

1. *Luke 22:24-26.*

    — What were the disciples arguing about (v. 24)?

    — To what did Jesus liken the disciple's attitude (v. 25)?

    — What way did Jesus suggest is to show greatness (v. 26)?

    — In what way did Jesus give these men an actual illustration of what He taught here, later that day (see John 13:1-17)?

2. *Luke 14:7-11.*

    — What were the guests doing that Jesus took note of (v. 7)?

    — What does Jesus recommend doing in a social situation where honor is being shown (v. 8-10)?

    — What universal law of social position did Jesus give (v. 11)?

3. *Philippians 2:3-11.*

- What motivations does the Bible exclude for any act (v. 3)?

- How are we to consider others in comparison to ourselves (v. 3)?

- Is it wrong to look after your own interests (v. 4)?

- What is our standard of attitudes related to ambition (v. 5)?

- What happened to Jesus as a result of His humbling himself (v. 6-11)?

4. *Scripture Search.* In each instance below name the person involved with their particular ambition.

- 2 Samuel 15:1-13; 18:18

- Esther 5:9-13

- Matthew 20:20-21

- 3 John 9

- Genesis 3:5-6

- Isaiah 14:12-15

5. *Personal Reflection.*

- What in your life might be termed "holy ambition"?

- What desire for achievement do you have which seems to you to be wholesome human aspiration?

- If selfish ambition were to creep into your desire for success, where might you notice it first?

6. *Personal Reflection.* What is one single thing you could do in response to the truths in this chapter?

- An action to take:

- A promise to make:

8
HONESTY:
Speaking Absolute Truth

Therefore each of you must put off falsehood and speak truthfully to his neighbor, for we are all members of one body.
—Ephesians 4:25

Remember your first lie? I was about five or six years old. An older boy from down the street led me off on a great exploration of the woods behind the park a few blocks from my house. My parents had forbidden me to go beyond a two-block limit. But Columbus, Magellan, and Marco Polo beckoned . . . off I went exploring uncharted territories. When I returned home my mother asked where I'd been. I lied.

Do you remember your first lie? More important than your first, have you been less than absolutely honest recently?

Lying is pervasive in our society. We have come first to admit, then accept, lying as necessary in our world. Governments lie as a matter of routine. As a teenager in 1960, I was wounded to discover that "Honest Ike" had lied to the world about Francis Gary Powers' U2 flight over Russia. My old war hero confessed to the world that he had lied . . . even defended it as "necessary" to protect his country's interests. I was disappointed . . . after all, as many good Christians, I had campaigned for Ike as an elementary school student!

Then came President Nixon who told some whoppers in his self-righteous sort of way. He came tumbling down through the efforts of two Washington Post reporters who practiced a number of lies and deceptions of their own as they tracked down the President's lies. Jody Powell now admits he lied about Carter's policies occasionally. And in the Iran-Contra scandal during the Reagan administration, lies were elevated by some to be judged heroic and quite necessary.

The CIA admits it has consistently lied, not only to other nations, but to their own citizens as well. In Vietnam the army lied about the body counts and the "victory at hand." The finest U.S. corporations regularly practice bribery in other nations. What has our standard of honesty in government come to?

Of course lying is not new . . . America's practice of breaking treaties with the native Americans is a shameful blot on its past. The truth is, we are a society of liars. We've even come to take lying lightheartedly. Several years ago, David Leisure climbed to fabulous fame and wealth by age 37 in Isuzu Motors $20 million TV "Liar Campaign." Joe Isuzu enthusiastically made preposterous verbal claims for the Isuzu cars while captions underneath him read "(He's lying)."

I remember taking my automobile to a church

member to get a quote on some body work. Worried about the expense, I asked "How much is this going to cost me?" His reply: "You gonna pay cash or do you need a receipt?" I needed a receipt and said so. His reply: "That'll cost you more – got to pay Uncle Sam ya know." Do Christians sometimes lie?

I remember one of my college professors asking and answering the aggravating question: "What's the major difference between an unsaved person and a Christian?" Her answer: "Ten years." Too often it seems to be so. The world's sinking standard of truth often creeps into the church body until we adopt the world's standards, only ten years later. Even ministers get caught in the web of truth-stretching and exaggeration. Is your church letting down the standard of absolute honesty? Are you hiding, stretching, or shading the truth?

Kinds of Lying

Most Christians would condemn a bold-faced lie. We are not likely to get caught telling such an outright falsehood. But there are other forms of lying which sometimes trip up the believer. Christians are more likely to be tempted to deliver *half-truths* – a partially true statement (which is also partially false). Or there is *flattery* – insincere praise. There are *false excuses* – not giving the real reason for your actions. There are *false impressions* when the actual words used are technically true, but you mean to give the hearer a totally different idea.

The Christian may be tempted to *exaggeration* – stretching facts and stories for effect. There is *deceit* – contriving a false reputation for yourself. Sometimes the believer may be tempted to *suppress the truth,* keeping silent when the truth is needed. I would hope no Christian would be guilty of *slander* – false stories told with the intention to harm. But he or she might be caught in a *white lie* – a falsehood told for a good cause. The devil is the father of lies and has been exceedingly creative in providing a varied choice of methods for the person who wishes to be less than absolutely honest.

This chapter will not deal with every kind of lying (though reading through the list in the foregoing paragraph may be a worthy repeat exercise). This chapter intends to focus on three areas where church folk – even ministers – are tempted to lie:

Lying about Numbers

How we love to stretch numbers. The church-growth movement has spawned some fine growth and success in churches. In our quest for success and local church fame, we try to grow and increase . . . if we can't, we sometimes take the easy shortcut to success – lying about numbers. Back in the days when church bus programs were at their height, I heard of one pastor who just couldn't get the bus attendance up to his predecessor's. He called across the country to find out his predecessor's secret. The answer: "Oh, I always added 50 to the total . . . you know, for the ones I might have missed."

Another pastor recently told me he examined the actual local records of his predecessor and compared them with what was reported to the district. He discovered as much as a 50% variance from week to week. A third young pastor wrote a heart-breaking letter reporting the sad story of how his predecessor has simply looked over the crowd each Sunday and said "Looks like a good Sunday, I'd say we have about 350 here today." No actual counting was done. The estimated attendance was reported for years to Church officials. The young new pastor had carefully counted people one by one. The records showed a precipitous drop of as many as a hundred people – yet the attenders said that the crowds seemed about the same or larger. He wrote, "I'm afraid people are going to say 'that young fellow went in there and simply ruined that church'."

"How many'd you have," is the standard question church people – especially ministers – ask each other. The pressure for a successful answer is high. Has your church become loose with the truth? One pastor's exaggeration had become such a laughing matter to his people that they secretly dubbed him "Pastor Pinocchio."

But it is not just ministers under success-pressure who sometimes lie. Church members are equally as bad. Sometimes the members "inflate" current numbers. But, more often, they magnify past numbers. One pastor was continually hounded by a fellow who frequently greeted him at the door with something like "Well, preacher, you had 155 today, but back there when Rev. Otis was here we ran over 200 every single Sunday . . . yep, those were great days." This pastor was so annoyed by the constant irritation, he drove to his district headquarters and dragged out the record books. The records showed that the church had never averaged over 200 for even one month, though they did have several big days when the attendance exceeded 200. Like yeast, the attendance had grown as the old fellow had let it rise in his mind over time.

Some Christian people kiddingly call this kind of numerical exaggeration "evangelistically speaking." What?! Have we become so dulled to honesty that we brazenly attach the sacred concept of "evangelistic" to this kind of truth-stretching? It is an awful abuse of "evangelistic." God prefers the more accurate term: *lying.* Lying is not evangelistic . . . it is devilish.

The church needs a renewed commitment to absolute honesty in numbers. Our yes should be yes and our no, no. And our 200 should be 200, not 178.

Lying About Accomplishments

This, too, is a snare for church people – lying

about what we've done in the past. Local church leaders are simply overwhelmed to discover that in a prospective candidate's last church "There were only 26 in the first service . . . and just last month he had 286." Wow! "Let's get this fellow here . . . maybe he can do that sort of thing for us."

What the leaders weren't told is that the fellow's first service was a midweek prayer meeting . . . (in August)! "Just last month" the 286 attendance was on Easter Sunday. They somehow got the impression that the *average* attendance has risen from 26 to 286. False impressions, if made intentionally, are lies.

Ministers in search of a new church often hide half-truths about accomplishments in their resumé. Sure, a resumé is supposed to present the record of a minister in the best possible light. But in our quest for honor it's easy to "puff" our accomplishments until they become outright lies.

But local church leaders are no better. When a new candidate is interviewed, the leaders frequently paint a far more rosy picture of the church and its people than is true. A pastor recently told me at lunch "The church purely and simply lied to me." Sure, you don't have to tell a candidate everything. But purposefully masking church problems, and willfully painting a rosier picture than is true, is clearly lying. (Of course, occasionally both are fooled by each other's deception. They may wind up getting each other . . . and both are disappointed!)

I have heard at least a dozen ministers say something like "I had no idea whatsoever what I was getting myself into . . . everything was painted rosy to me." And not a few members have said, after a messy situation had developed with their pastor, "We had no idea he had this problem, but now we find out this happened twice before at other churches . . . *now* they tell us!"

False towers of accomplishments eventually

tumble down. In 1985 I happened to be in Arizona when "Duke" Tully, publisher of the *Arizona Republic,* collapsed amidst a pile of lies. He was an exciting man, with quite a wallop in Arizona politics. He had been rejected by the Air Force, but loved planes, so he joined the Civil Air Patrol. I suppose he imagined himself as a great pilot, and soon began claiming so to others. He eventually invented a heroic war record for himself. He convinced everyone that he had flown more than 100 missions in Vietnam, and had been awarded a number of military decorations including the Purple Heart and Flying Cross. It was all fictitious.

After everything came out into the open he resigned as publisher. His own paper printed his verbatim remarks: "It just built and built, and suddenly I was under an avalanche and could not get out of it. As I moved up the ladder, it just snowballed and got away from me."

Lies about our accomplishments can eventually become such a part of our own psyche that we can come to believe them ourselves. Total reality breakdown is then not far behind.

Not too long after the fall of "Duke" Tully, one of my associates came tumbling down too. A Christian college president had concocted a similar list of accomplishments including an inflated military record, a manufactured Ph.D. and several other educational accomplishments. Many of these things he had come to believe about himself! And his motives were good . . . it had all been done "for a good cause" – the institution *needed* a hero. But, once the truth came out, the leader sneaked away in shame. The work reeled. The college took years to recover from this leader's dishonesty, to say nothing of the disappointed hero-worshipers, many of them young people. Some of these may never fully recover.

Why do we inflate our accomplishments? We think we have to impress people. We're afraid that the bare truth just isn't outstanding, interesting, or comical enough. So we embellish our past in an attempt to impress and entertain others. *But others know it!* The lie detector provides more evidence of what Christians have known all along – you can tell when someone is lying. Sure, there are hidden physical signs . . . increased heartbeat, perspiration, imperceptible changes in breathing measured by the polygraph.

But there are visible open signs too: voice tone, eye movement, and body gestures. These outward signs are picked up by listeners. The listener's subconscious mind collects and processes all this data and feeds a mental impression to the listener's mind . . . "he's lying." Incredible! People carry their own lie detectors around with them! When someone is inflating their accomplishments, others can sense it. Perhaps they can't prove it, but for some reason or another they don't feel they can trust this story. It is their own inner polygraph telling them not to trust the person speaking.

Do you lie about your accomplishments? It is time for Christian people to start telling the truth, the whole truth, and nothing but the truth . . . especially when it comes to our past accomplishments. The church should be a place where we accept and affirm each other as people of worth with or without fantastic past accomplishments. It is time to reduce pressure for success on pastors, so they can quit feeling compelled to lie about their record. Would you really rather have a successful liar for a pastor than a mediocre honest pastor? Let's tell the truth about past accomplishments.

Lying in Stories and Illustrations

Am I ever meddling now. I know the acceptable speaker's routine . . . dig around a bit to get ideas. Listen to a couple of tapes and read a few books. Then a teacher or speaker "makes it his own" by developing illustrations similar to the ones read or heard.

This is a realistic plan, but it is full of danger. The danger? Counterfeit illustrations! Face it, some of our lives just aren't that interesting. Or at least we don't see the illustrations in everyday life like others do. The speaker's temptation is to make up a similar story based on fact – taking a true experience and embellishing it a bit. Invent a few additional lines of narrative. Embellish the story by tossing in a few extra "facts" and soon you've got a great illustration. After all, it keeps the listeners awake . . . it's all for a good cause, isn't it?

Many years ago I had the opportunity to travel from camp to camp during one summer. One particular preacher had an itinerary which crisscrossed mine. The first time I heard his message on evangelism, it was glorious . . . he told how he had witnessed to a fellow "in the plane on the way out here yesterday." The fellow hadn't made a decision, but "you could tell he was under conviction." He even had given the speaker his address and promised to start attending church. I was impressed with this message on evangelism. So were the people. Here was a speaker who really practiced what he preached – he was calling us to witness, and he had done it the day before on the plane!

At a later camp I ran into this speaker again and he told the story again. This time he added the line that big tears were running down the prospect's cheeks. Perhaps he'd forgotten that detail in the first telling? People loved it! There was a big altar response – people wanting to share their faith like this man.

Anyway, by the end of the summer, the tale had grown so tall that he had the fellow receiving Christ, with several people around them crying as the onlookers also expressed interest in receiving Christ. "We had a prayer meeting right there in that plane" he tearfully said as he closed his sermon with this illustration. The people fervently applauded. The only trouble: the story was a lie. By the end of summer I wondered if the first story was even true. This fellow was practicing "preacher perjury." We all would condemn this kind of pastoral lying. Wouldn't we?

But do *you* lie? What about those little "white lies?" Do you decorate your stories? How about that hunting tale of that 12-point buck? Do you lie about your age? When was the last time you listed or told someone your weight? Was it true? Do you tell stories of your military days? College days? Are they true? Are you a fisherman? What about that four-mile walk you took to school each day as a child . . . was it *really* four miles? Are these innocent exaggerations? God doesn't think so. God figures His children should tell the simple unadulterated truth. Forked tongues belong in the serpent's family, not God's.

The church – especially we who are speakers – should renew our commitment to honesty in stories and illustrations. Let's make a fresh start at truthful storytelling . . . even if our friends or audiences go to sleep. As ministers and members, we must put off all manner of lying, and start to speak the absolute truth to each other. We must "speak the truth in love." There is nothing "loving" about lying.

Now what about *you,* my friend?

All I ask you to do is listen. If you are married, be sure to *listen to your spouse.* After one great ministerial liar was exposed I always wondered, "Where was his wife?" She traveled with him often and certainly knew he was lying. Didn't she say anything to him? Perhaps she thought, "God's using him so, I'd better keep quiet . . ." Or maybe she spoke up and he refused to listen. I don't know. But I do know my wife monitors my speaking (and writing) carefully. If I stretch a fact or story, she says so. And, I listen. You should too. If your husband or wife corrects a figure, or a story, take it like a Christian. It might keep you from becoming an even bigger liar.

More important, *listen to the Holy Spirit.* Is your heart pricked about your own looseness with truth? Do you sense a correction or rebuke from Him about your truthfulness? If so, you know what to do . . . repent. Listen to that "still, small voice" inside you. Do *you* hear any admonition from the Spirit? If so, listen.

The next time you are tempted to stretch a number, or inflate your past accomplishments, or embellish an illustration to make it more interesting . . . remember *what you are is more important than what you say.* It is better to be known as having a lackluster record of accomplishments, or as a dull and uninteresting conversationalist than to be known as an untrustworthy liar.

Some Questions to Ponder

INSTRUCTIONS: Prayerfully answer the questions using the following key:

T = TRUE of me, sorry to say.
F = FALSE, this is not true for me.
? = QUESTION, I need to think more about this.

_____ I sometimes say "I'd love to come, but I can't make it," when I really could make it.

_____ I sometimes tell people "I was sick" when I really wasn't.

_____ I sometimes quietly pocket extra cash received "conveniently forgetting" to report it for taxes.

_____ When someone asks "Do you know so and so?" I sometimes say yes when I don't know the person.

_____ I sometimes lie about my weight to other people.

_____ My past tax returns are not totally true and accurate.

_____ I sometimes say "the check is in the mail" but it isn't.

_____ When a person asks "Have you read such and such book?" I sometimes say that I have when I really haven't.

_____ My spouse sometimes corrects the facts in my stories.

_____ I sometimes say "Sure I remembered that" when I had totally forgotten until they reminded me.

_____ I sometimes say "Sorry I'm late, I was held up" but I really wasn't held up.

_____ I tend to inflate attendance and financial numbers.

_____ I tend to twist verses to support what I believe.

_____ My resumé is totally honest . . . even if the national press were to comb it today, nothing is stretched or inflated.

_____ I sometimes say "I've been praying for you," when I haven't.

_____ I sometimes give the impression that I give more to the church than I really do.

_____ I admit a tendency to "beef up" stories, stretching the truth to get a better response.

_____ I sometimes tell a "technical truth" which still leaves a false impression to the hearer.

_____ I sometimes flatter people, dishing out false praise to them.

_____ I sometimes keep quiet when I hear a lie, suppressing the truth, becoming an accessory to another's lie.

_____ I sometimes compliment people when I really don't feel that way.

_____ I sometimes act like I'm far more busy than I really am.

_____ I sometimes even lie to myself and to God . . . for instance, I think I may have lied to myself as I answered some of these questions.

Now go back over the list and circle any God seems to be correcting you about.

Bible Study

1. Genesis 20:1-17. Why did Abraham tell this half-truth? What should he have done? Can you think of an example today when a Christian might be tempted to tell a half-truth?

2. *Acts 5:1-11.* Of what kind of lying were Ananias and Sapphira guilty? Why were they punished so severely . . . does it seem like God overreacted?

3. *John 4:16-18.* In what way was the Samaritan woman's answer to Jesus technically true, and in what ways was it a lie? Give an example of a technical truth in today's world which can also be a lie?

4. *Ephesians 4:15.*

— Certainly we are to speak the truth . . . but this verse places a restriction on how we are to speak it. What is that restriction?

— Give several examples of how something truthful can be said in a wrong way, at a wrong time, or with the wrong motive.

5. *Proverbs 12:22.* Describe God's attitude toward lies.

6. *Proverbs 21:6.* Rewrite this verse in your own words as it applies to a modern business or sales person.

7. *Revelation 21:8.* List the eight kinds of people from this verse on the left side of the following space. On the right side, write in their destiny.

8. *Colossians 3:9.* What do you think the term "old self" means in this verse? What might it have to do with lying?

9. *Personal Reflection.* What is one single thing you could do in response to the truth of this chapter?

— An action to take is

— A promise to make is

9
PEACEMAKING:
Mending Broken Relationships

Peacemakers who sow in peace raise a harvest of righteousness.
—James 3:18

Peacemakers are supposed to be "blessed" according to the Sermon on the Mount. But what is a peacemaker? How am I to "make peace" or "sow peace?" Where am I to do it? Why am I to do it?

Peacemaking is an uncommon discipline of holy living. Though the prescription for healing division is just plain common sense – and we already know it, *obeying* God's recommendations for peacemaking is where we have trouble.

How division develops

No two snowflakes – and no two people are alike. God is a God of orderliness, but not of uniformity. His creation is one of infinite variety. His crowning creation, man, is especially varied. Humanity represents a broad "spectrum" of assorted fascinating personalities, temperaments, and racial and ethnic traits.

Some of us are shy and passive, while others are outgoing and aggressive. Some are sensitive and emotional, while others, are logical, never letting their feelings show. Some of us are orderly, organized, neat perfectionists. The rest of us are messy, disorganized, and forgetful.

Differences cause interpersonal friction. Friction occurs in interpersonal relationships when we spend time with people different from ourselves. The shy, ingrown person is irritated by the outgoing, boisterous, noisy person. The orderly person thinks the disorganized person is a slob. Energetic hard-drivers think easygoing people are lazy wimps. The easygoing person returns the assessment, considering the hard-driver a fascist dictator who runs roughshod over everyone who gets in his way.

When interpersonal friction occurs, we tend to see another's personality strength as a weakness. The neat are considered "fastidious." Bold people are considered "brash." Sensitive folk are termed "touchy." The humorous become "silly," the cautious are "fearful," and the frugal become "skinflints." The strengths of others become the very targets of our criticism. Nowhere is this seen so clearly as in marriage. Differences cause friction.

We have mentioned only personality traits thus far. What of differing opinions on politics, theology, music, or religious convictions? What of differing personal preferences like when a sensible person ought to go to bed, what one should eat (or not eat) for breakfast? Which way should the toilet paper hang on the dispenser? The possibilities for interpersonal friction are immeasurable! Friction is to be expected in interpersonal relationships. We are to treat these irritations with grace and acceptance, overlooking the irritations. Friction is not sin. The next step is the fatal one.

Friction can cause broken relationships. Constant friction can lead to relational breakdown. If we do not learn to deal with friction appropriately, it will slowly drive a wedge between relationships so that we eventually "break fellowship" with another. One starts to avoid the other. Perhaps both dodge each other. The two begin leaving by separate doors and avoid mutual friends. Eventually each gathers several sympathetic friends, and factions form – people take "sides" in the battle. Ultimately the whole group may be destroyed, simply because the initial broken relationship between two good people wasn't faced and repaired. Have you ever witnessed the battlefield of such a broken relationship? Have you ever seen a whole church eventually destroyed because two or more of God's people didn't make peace?

How can we avoid this senseless slaughter? A quarrel, like a fire, can be quenched early with a pint of water. Let go, it will rage out of control, eventually consuming everything in its path.

There are four different situations where relational breakdown is possible. Each has its own prescription. The first: when someone has wronged me. Second: when someone else feels I've wronged them. Third: when others are quarreling and I'm not even involved. Fourth: when the whole church is divided into factions.

What to do . . .

I. When someone has wronged me.

What do you do when you've got a grievance

against another Christian? Maybe they said something harsh and cut you deeply. Perhaps they pulled a procedural "end run" play in a committee meeting and you were omitted from an important assignment you really wanted. What should you do when the pastor pulls a fast one and works you out of the job you've held for seventeen years in your church? How should you respond when someone tells you one of your "friends" told them a bit of gossip about you that morning? What is a Christian supposed to do when he feels he's been wronged? This simple four-step process for reconciliation when someone hurts you works. It is a time-honored plan, and if you follow it, you'll get things straightened out most every time.

1. Arrange for a private talk. Take action. Immediately. Don't brood and churn about it any longer. Feeling you've been treated unjustly is the breeding ground for bitterness, a cancer of the soul. This malignancy will grow and spread its tentacles rapidly. So, don't wait. Take action. Go and see the one you feel has offended you face-to-face.

In such a private encounter the offender is more likely to confess and restore the relationship. Once others are involved the stakes get higher and confession is slower to come. Go directly to the person. Don't write a letter. A letter can easily be misconstrued or misunderstood. Go alone and try to straighten this out just between the two of you.

Of course you must be careful in approaching the individual. Don't be accusatory. Obviously you shouldn't say, "I heard you told a lie about me and I've come to see if you did." Merely share why *you* feel hurt, offering them an opportunity to minister to your hurt. Never go in anger. Calm down first. But don't wait more than a day either. Going in anger may be better than not going at all. Make sure you approach with tenderness. After all, you are attempting to extract a splinter from your brother's eye. Such an operation requires considerable adroitness.

The point: *take action.* Don't wait. Arrange a private talk with the person who hurt you. Explain to them why you are offended and tell them you need to "clear the air" between you. In 90% of all cases when this advice is followed, the individual will respond positively, and you have restored the relationship before it deteriorates. But, what about the 10% which still do not yield a reconciliation, even after your one-on-one talk? For the remaining 10% there is a second step.

2. Take a few others and try again. If you didn't settle the issue between you the first time, take one or two others along and go again. Pick a few Christians who are wise, gracious, and highly respected. Obviously you should not get a hand-picked flock of your own friends who will side with you automatically. You need to choose impartial, discerning, spiritually minded Christians. Let these mature mediators lead the discussion. Place yourself under their leadership and listen to their counsel and correctives.

This introduction of several impartial, mature believers often completely changes the atmosphere. The two of you in conflict will easily "work it out" under their leadership, repairing your relationship. Well, maybe not in every case. Perhaps in a remaining 1% of the time you try the second step it won't bring reconciliation. In these cases one out of a hundred, there is even a third step.

3. Take it to the church. After all, who ought to settle disputes between Christians . . . secular courts? When all private attempts at reconciliation have failed, we should turn to the church. Who is better able to mediate your dispute than mature leaders of a church? They have a greater interest in relationships than results. If your first two attempts have failed to produce a repaired relationship, take it to the church's leadership to whom both of you are accountable. Commit yourselves to live by the decision of the leaders on the matter. If you and your brother are not involved in the same church, then agree together on a panel to decide the issue between you. If you can't even agree on this, select one mature leader each, then let these two select the third. The point is that when two Christians are deadlocked, the church leaders should decide the outcome of the dispute.

These three steps will solve 99.9% of all interpersonal disputes. But, what of the one-tenth of one percent of the situations left? Suppose the church leaders have decided in your favor, but your brother still refuses to give in? He remains stubborn and inflexible. What then are we to do? There is yet hope – a *fourth* step.

4. Forget it! That's right! Simply and quickly dismiss the whole affair. Don't get bitter, get better! Don't brood over his or her refusal to give in. Give up on trying to recover your loss or gain a just settlement. Simply forget it. Maybe he or she is not even a real "brother" or "sister" after all. If they are a pagan at heart, treat them like any other pagan – hope and pray for their salvation, but don't hang around them. Simply dismiss the whole affair. Treat the person like you would a tax collector. When the first three steps have failed, forget the whole thing, and get on with your life.

To most of us all this elaborate system seems unnecessary. We'd rather go to "Caesar's court" to settle disputes over money or marriage. Or we don't even try to repair broken relationships. It seems easier to simply break the relationship than to follow this four-step process. We're too busy for all this. "I don't need him (or her) anyway," we say. But we are wrong. This intricate process is designed because God values interpersonal relationships, especially marriage. It is because a broken relationship is so serious to God that He expects us to go to these ends to repair the fracture.

So if you feel someone has cheated you, hurt you, been unfair to you . . . set up a meeting between the two of you and see if you can clear it up. Start this four-step process – having a peaceful relationship is worth the effort.

What to do . . .

II. When someone thinks I've wronged them.

Have you ever sensed that someone was holding something against you? You just *knew* that a particular person had bad feelings about you. Perhaps you didn't even know why, but you knew it just the same. When a Christian feels this way, what are we to do?

Or, perhaps you discover another's bad feelings toward you through a third party. Several years ago a good friend approached me and told me how one particular fellow was absolutely furious at me. He was angered by what I had said on a certain committee. He knew how I eventually voted and was steamed. My friend encouraged me to go and see this fellow while his anger was still hot. It didn't seem wise to me at first. "Let him cool down," I thought to myself, "then I'll go." But I knew better. It is better to deal with hot anger than smoldering bitterness. So I went. I opened the conversation like this:

> "I've come to see you because I think I've offended you. We may not be able to agree about what I said or how I voted, but we can't have a broken relationship over this or anything else. So I've come to see what I can do to clear the air between us. I love you as a brother and want to keep our relationship right. Can we talk about it?"

In this case the man was "easily entreated." We spent several hours talking, sometimes emotionally, sometimes quietly. We traced our relationship and several tender bruises we had given each other in the past. He shared an unrelated personal crisis he was going through which I knew nothing about. We tried repeatedly to come to agreement on the particular issue, but never did. We still disagree. But, though we disagree, we understand each other better. Most important of all, we have restored our relationship. That time ended with a tearful hug, and we continue to consider each other with high esteem to this day.

I had learned an important lesson. It is hard – perhaps impossible – to come to agreement with everybody. But, it *is* possible to keep the relationship going in most cases.

The advice is simple. If you sense someone has something against you, go to them and try to work it out. Go even if you think you are right, or you know they are being immature and petty. Go to them if the incident was purposeful or accidental, actual or supposed. Take action. Go clear the air between you.

It's fascinating how God works "the ends against the middle" on these kinds of things. If someone has hurt me, I'm to go to *them*. And they are supposed to come to *me*. Both of us are instructed to fix the relationship. If either one obeys, the relationship can be repaired. This is how important relationships are to God. Whether you are hurt, or the one who did the hurting, you are supposed to go to the other and fix it up.

Sometimes neither follows this advice. Occasionally two believers end up at odds with each other and neither attempts to go to the other one. What should we do when two other Christians are fighting and self-righteously refusing to "bury the hatchet."

What to do...

When others are quarreling.

Suppose several people in your church are fussing, and you are not even involved. "Mind your own business," right? That's the conventional wisdom. We tell our children, "Keep your nose out of other people's business." We follow this advice ourselves. When others get into a church scrap, we often stand by as sanctimonious spectators. "Let them alone," we smugly say, "they'll settle it between themselves." And if either of them followed the peacemaking plans above, they would. But they don't. So we stand by as the flames of fractured relationships blaze hotter and consume marriages, friendships, even entire churches. We say, "Let's remember them in prayer." We fiddle around while the city of God burns.

There's a pattern to all advice on broken relationships: get involved. Broken relationships, like broken bones, don't "go away if you give them time." Churches that have not settled past broken relationships are now permanently crippled in their ministry. Broken bones often need "setting" for them to heal. Broken relationships need "setting" too.

When two or more people in a Christian community get on the "outs," the rest of us are to pitch in to fix it. We together are the Body of Christ... each a particular part. Can the hand say, "Who cares if the heart and lungs break fellowship, let them settle it themselves... it's not our business." If the vital organs of a body cease to function in concert, soon the hand too will be blue, cold and dead.

Any break in relationship in the Body *is* our business! We all are to work at fixing the fracture. That is not to say that we are to descend on the pair of quarreling people like a cloud of locusts. Common sense and good judgment are in order. The pastor of the church often coordinates this kind of thing. The most mature Christians — the most spiritually minded – will be the ones called on for the delicate task of repairing broken relationships.

Why do we often ignore this sensible advice? Why does the church sit sweetly singing every Sunday when we know there are two believers among us with an unseen war raging between them? Why do we stand idly by as homes are being ripped apart by broken relationships? Why don't we make an effort to restore these breaking relationships? Because we are scared. We don't want to get dirty. We don't want to take sides. So, we do nothing. Thus, we sadly watch friendships, marriages, even entire churches go swirling down the drain because of fractured relationships. "Rescuing the perishing" should begin at home!

God has a better plan: get involved. When relationships start unraveling, the church is supposed to help these believers make peace. We are to get them back together again. This is "peacemaking." It is getting involved. Taking time. Helping to repair that relationship about to go through the shredder. It is getting your hands dirty and your ego battered in even the messiest of messes.

And when you do get involved you mustn't take sides. And don't always hope for a quick fix – these things take time. Gently, tenderly "set the bone" of this fracture, then give it time to heal. This is what Christ expects of you. Even if you fail at the whole attempt, even if you fumble and things turn worse, He wants *you* to lovingly, carefully, compassionately *get involved* when others are quarreling.

If you don't follow this advice your whole church will become divided into factions. Then the problem will require even more drastic measures to correct.

What to do . . .

When the whole church is divided.

Men and women are social creatures. We automatically draw others into the net of our actions and attitudes. What starts out as a simple difference produces friction. This friction eventually can produce a fracture in relationships. Now two people are openly or silently at odds. But injustice loves company. Soon others are drawn into the web and two "sides" form. Eventually the entire church or group disintegrates into factions.

In the Civil War, following the battle of Chancellorsville, the rear guard of Stuart's cavalry sounded the alarm that Union troops were attacking. The first and third Virginia regiments promptly charged each other, killing many. Like the troops, sometimes we forget who the enemy is. We turn on our allies and begin lobbing shells into their camp. The worst wounds in the church community are self-inflicted.

What if you are attending a church deeply divided into factions? Maybe one group follows the "founding pastor" of your church who has recently retired. In their mind no one can match *his* abilities and anointing. Maybe another faction has rallied around a fellow in your church who has a gifted personality and a magnetic charisma. This leader has such wisdom, eloquence, wit and intellectual keenness. He's dynamic! He's fantastic! He's _____! But he is also "anathema" to the faction following Rev. "Founding Pastor." And there's the rub.

Maybe you even have a third group – the conservative reactionaries, traditionalists. They are distressed that the church is "letting down the old standard." They wonder if some of the new Christians are even truly Christian. They think the solution to everything is getting back to the "old paths." Perhaps you even have a fourth group – a super-spiritual group who is wholly disgusted with these baby, weak Christians fussing and fighting with each other. This clique considers themselves "above it all" and whispers to each other, "Isn't it just terrible, the way *they* act?" They thank God that they are true followers of Christ and not mere men.

Such factions may adopt leaders who are totally unaware that they are the "heroes" of said factions. Have you ever seen this kind of a divided church? What would (or should) you do if you ever become a part of one?

Get help! Once broken relationships have deteriorated into factions and discord, hope and help must come from outside the group. Factions won't settle their own disputes. There are too many people – and interests – involved. No settlement will satisfy everybody. Your only hope is to go outside your church. There you must get help. A divided church needs an outside authority. It should be someone all sides accept as spiritual and wise, and to whom all will submit their wills. Such a factioned church needs an "apostle" – one with God's authority and wisdom. This kind of apostolic ministry may fall to a wise old spiritual monarch in the denomination, or it could be an elected official. Whoever it is, it must be a man or woman of wisdom and insight who is willing to get involved as a judge.

The church now submits itself to a sort of "binding arbitration" with the outside authority sitting as judge. After hearing enough to discern the essence of the problem, he or she retires to seek God's wisdom. When the decision is rendered it is final – all sides submit to it.

Doesn't this plan make better sense than the alternatives? Isn't it better than letting strife destroy the church? Doesn't this plan make better sense than Christians dragging their complaints against each other into a secular court to be decided by a pagan?

Is your church divided into factions? Rather than hoping that someone in the church will emerge as the savior, seek an outside wise leader. Surrender the decision to him. Who knows? Picking such an arbitrator may be the first thing in years to which you can get everyone to agree.

Now what about you, my friend?

Can you think of someone somewhere whom you are holding something against? Or has God reminded you of someone who seems to be holding something against *you?* Have you thought of some third parties – several other people who are breaking fellowship with each other? What should you do? If God is convicting you about any of these things follow His advice: *Take action.* Go to the one you may have hurt, or to the one who hurt you. Get involved in helping others who seem to have an unraveling relationship. And if your whole church is in a mess, start campaigning to recruit a wise outside authority to judge you.

Do you know of a broken relationship? A *breaking* relationship? Will you take the action necessary to sow the seeds of peacemaking? If you do, *you* will reap a great and satisfying harvest of righteousness!

Bible Study

1. Matthew 18:15-17.

   – With which of the four categories of broken relationships does this scripture deal (v. 15)?

   ____ When someone has wronged me
   ____ When someone thinks I have wronged them
   ____ When others are quarreling
   ____ When the whole church is divided

- Describe in your own words the four-step procedure for repairing this kind of broken relationship:

2. Matthew 5:23-24.

- With which of the four categories of broken relationships does this scripture deal (v. 23)?

    ____ When someone has wronged me
    ____ When someone feels I have wronged them
    ____ When others are quarreling
    ____ When the whole church is divided

- What action are we to take when this kind of fracture occurs?

- What is *not* a substitute for right relationships with our brother or sister?

3. Philippians 4:2-3.

   – With which of the four categories of broken relationships does this scripture deal?

   _____ When someone has wronged me
   _____ When someone thinks I have wronged them
   _____ When others are quarreling
   _____ When the whole church is divided

4. 1 Corinthians 1:10-12.

   – With which of the four categories of broken relationships does this scripture deal?

   _____ When someone has wronged me
   _____ When someone feels I have wronged them
   _____ When others are quarreling
   _____ When the whole church is divided

   – Review the description of a modern, divided church in the section, "When the Whole Church is Divided." Can you match up the modern examples of factions with the four factions in the Corinthian church?

   A charismatic personality/dynamic speaker
   B founding pastor
   C conservative/traditionalists
   D super-spiritual/above it all

   _____ "Of Paul" faction.

   _____ "Of Apollos" faction

   _____ "Of Cephas" faction

   _____ "Of Christ" faction

5. *Titus 3:10.* Differences alone are enough to cause the friction leading to broken relationships. However, sometimes a church or group has a person in it who delights in causing division and discord. Such people savor the excitement of a big fight and delight in stirring up quarrels. In this scripture a three-step method is prescribed for dealing with such people. What are those three steps?

— Step one

— Step two

— Step three

6. *Ephesians 4:3.*

— "Making" peace or "bringing back" unity is what we are to do when things go wrong. However, what even better plan does this verse suggest?

7. *Romans 15:5-6.*

– A spirit of unity is what the church seeks in its effort at peacemaking. We must do our part, in working at reconstructing broken relationships. However, where does the church ultimately get its unity?

8. *1 Peter 3:8.* If you viewed your church as a unified orchestra attempting to produce beautiful "harmony," what insights would that idea give to each of the following:

– Competition

– Solos

– Sections . . . brass, wind . . .

– the Conductor

– Melody vs. harmony

– Individual vs. group effort

9. Personal reflection. Using your own abbreviations or personal writing code, list below any broken relationships you may need to mend:

— Someone who wronged me

— Someone who feels I have wronged them

— Others who have deteriorating relationships

— Entire churches or groups divided into factions

10. Personal Reflection. What is one single thing you could do in response to the truth of this chapter? Is there a promise you want to make to God?

— An action to take:

— A promise to make:

10
WHAT
to do
When Your Light
is Brighter Than
Your Life

Now to him who is able to do immeasurably more than all we ask or imagine, according to his power that is at work within us.
—Ephesians 3:20

We started this book off with a focus on "walking in the light." We outlined the ways God seems to help Christians change, by first giving them "light" on something in their lives that needs changed . . . put off or put on. Following this "dawning awareness" comes the Holy Spirit's work in producing a "growing conviction" that we must change. We said that when we make a "crisis decision" to change, relying on God's power, He grants "changing grace" to us and then it is our job to keep walking obediently by "disciplined obedience." This is how we "walk in the light."

But what happens when your light is brighter than your life? What are you to do when you clearly see areas in your life out of God's will? What should you do when you know of several qualities and practices clearly missing from your life which a good Christian ought to be and do? What do you do when you've got more light than you can walk in? What do you do when you can't seem to keep up with the light? Like Paul on the Damascus road, do you feel blinded and incapacitated by the light? Is it overwhelming?

Perhaps this book hasn't helped. Chapter after chapter we have examined biblical disciplines of holy living. You may have winced as you read. Perhaps you would read a chapter then sigh and admit you weren't living up to it. When you hurried to the next you only discovered one more area where you fell short. Maybe by now you are ready to give up? If so, this chapter is for you.

If you are feeling overwhelmed by the light, these eight thoughts may be just what you need to hear:

1. Don't Forget

The devil hangs around Christian folk a lot. He is always looking for a way to keep you from stepping forward in the new light God grants to you. His first ploy is to get you to forget the light. If Satan can divert our attention from the truth for a few days, or maybe a week or two . . . like the birds in the parable of the sower, Satan snatches away the truth before it finds root and conviction begins to grow (Matthew 13).

We are the devil's greatest ally in this strategy. We are so busy, scurrying here and there, trying to keep all the loose ends of our lives from falling apart, that we give truth little time to root and grow.

Most Christians spend most of their lives at the "dawning awareness" stage of spiritual growth, hearing truth they should obey then quickly forgetting it only to hear another truth which is also soon forgotten.

Sunday school classes don't help in this matter. We study a spiritual discipline, attitude or Christian behavior this week, then rapidly move on to another the next week with little attention given to actually implementing change. Light piles up week after week with little opportunity to change. And we preachers don't help either. We seldom stick with a topic long enough to allow listeners to assimilate permanent change in their lives. Week by week we approach new topics, recommending new attributes or habits listeners "ought'" to have. Then before there is a chance to change, we scurry on to the next topic.

Many Christians simply get into the forgetting habit. Week after week new light comes our way. It pricks our consciences a bit when we first hear it. But taking little time to ponder it, and even less time for prayer or introspection it soon dims and disappears. By Tuesday Satan has snatched Sunday's truth away.

Forgetting may seem like a solution to the bright-light problem. Simply forget the light and it will gradually fade. But this dangerous route produces an infantile faith. The light-conviction-obedience-change-light cycle is your only hope of spiritual maturity. Short-circuiting this process by quickly forgetting light produces a Christian life "stuck" in its progress. Many Christians have become hardened to truth. They forget the light soon after leaving their local church, or finishing a new book. Some whole churches are like this. They gather every week to take a "light shower," but the light is really not considered seriously. These become hearers only and not doers of the word.

So if your light is brighter than your life, don't

run from the light – it is your hope for growth. Don't dismiss the light in the hustle of life – it is your stability. And by all means remember the light – it is your route to spiritual growth.

2. Always "Keep on Keeping on"

If Satan can't get you to forget the light, he turns to his back-up plan – using it to discourage you. He is constantly searching for a way to turn good into evil. When he watches you gaining great new insights and reading and hearing more about God's standards of holiness, he plots a way to twist the good toward evil. His most useful scheme is to suggest to you that this light simply shows what a horrible Christian you really are. Just as the Holy Spirit has access to our minds, Satan can also introduce ideas into our thoughts. "See . . . if you were a *real* Christian you'd be doing all these things" he says. Except he seldom speaks in a third person voice: that is, "if *you* . . . *you'd* be doing." No, that would be too easy to spot. Rather Satan introduces thoughts to our minds in the first person singular tense: "If *I* were a real Christian *I'd* be doing all these things. It's as if we're talking to ourselves.

Soon we are entertaining Satan's thoughts. They come first as an idea, but as we ponder the concept we *receive* them . . . we take possession of them: "True, I *am* a pretty poor Christian . . . and I've never been able to really live it like I should . . . perhaps I should throw in the towel." As we ponder these thoughts we gradually adopt the enemy's proposal and begin to accept failure as a Christian.

Ironic, isn't it? The glorious light God sends your way – which comes with health, cheer, and hope – is twisted by Satan to produce discouragement, fear, and despair. The light God intended to prompt anticipation and a positive expectation, now yields apprehension and doubt. These are the ways of the Evil One. In his first temptation he twisted

God's words to Eve. Now he twists God's light to you.

So what should you do? Refuse to entertain Satan's thoughts. Develop the skill of recognizing this ploy of the devil. When these thoughts come to you which suggest giving up, ask yourself . . . "Now, can this be from God?" When the answer is "no" then attribute resignation thoughts to Satan.

So if your light is brighter than your life, and you're tempted to give up, don't let your knees buckle. Stand firm. Keep on keeping on. Hang in there. Refuse to succumb to Satan's tricks. Reject the devil's suggestion to capitulate. Don't give up!

3. Don't pretend

If the devil fails to get you to forget the truth, then fails at getting you to give up, he has a reserve maneuver in his bag of tricks – inducing you to pretend obedience. Of all the devil's devices this is his most devastating. Rather than go through all this tedious growth process, simply pretend you already obey this light. It took demonic genius to invent this idea! It's the busy person's ultimate answer to spiritual growth. Simply *act* like these truths are something you long ago came to practice. Discuss these disciplines in a Sunday school class like you've practiced them for ages. Nod knowingly as the pastor preaches on things you've never even tried. Wag your head sternly when some sin is being discussed – as if you've never even been tempted in this area.

Presto! You have instant spirituality. Or at least others think so. And, after all, isn't that what's most important – what others think? You get all this by simply pretending that your life is already way up there with all this light.

Whole congregations of Christians have opted to pretend holiness. No one ever admits to any sin or even temptation. All the testimonies report victory and triumph. Everybody seems perfect here.

What a wonderful congregation! Pretend holiness. What a brilliant solution!

Or is it? What does it produce? It makes you a hypocrite. You have to live with yourself – and you know your holiness is counterfeit. And the people closest to you know, too. Whole generations of children have been lost to the Kingdom because they saw through their parent's phony holiness. You might be able to fool some of the people some of the time, but you can't fool all of the people all of the time. Sooner or later they'll see your spiritual fraud. And you can seldom fool yourself. You know down deep inside what you really are, and you'll despise yourself for this deception. And you can never fool God. He sees your heart. He knows the real you. His Son spent hours condemning the Pharisees for this very sin – spiritual hypocrisy.

So if your light is brighter than your life, don't pretend holiness as a solution. Don't masquerade as an obedient person if you're not. God despised the prayer of the man who gave thanks for his great spiritual victories in comparison to others. But He welcomed the man who prayed "God be merciful to me, a sinner" (Luke 18:13). Reject the temptation to pretend obedience. You can become the person God intended you to be. But pretending won't get you there.

4. Look Back/Look Ahead

One of Satan's devices is to get you to look only at your present state and then gleefully suggest, "Look what a poor Christian you are." If you keep focusing on the present alone, you'll feel continually defeated. The best way to beat this attack is to spend more time looking back and ahead. Look back at what you were in the past. Compare that with what you are now. As you praise God for how much He's done to change you already, your faith begins to grow for the future. Simply assume God will continue to change you in the future at the rate He has in the past! Then focus again on the present with renewed confidence.

You may not be everything you should be, but you're a lot different than you were! And you can be assured that you will keep becoming more like Jesus if you submit to God's changing grace, for that is God's will for your life.

So if your light is brighter than your life, and you are discouraged by your spiritual progress, look back at how far you've come, then project ahead at how far you could go. That will supply you with the nerve to look at your present state with confidence that God can change you even now.

5. Make sure your light is from God

It is possible to get under a "human conviction." Sometimes you can fall under the shadow of some other person who impresses their own "convictions" on you. It could be a teacher, a pastor, a mature saint in the church, or the author of this book! You begin to think that you should stop or start doing something just because someone else has. This "human light" condemns you because you do not measure up to someone else's standards. This condemnation is not from the Holy Spirit. Your job is to obey God, not someone else's light.

The problem is telling the difference between God's conviction and human conviction. If you are not regularly looking into God's Word, it's easy to start getting your light from other people. "This person says Christians ought to . . ." Or "I heard on a Christian radio program the other day that Christians shouldn't . . ." Or maybe "I read this book and the author thinks that every Christian ought to . . ."

If you start down the road of listening to human conviction you will pile up a mountainous burden of "false guilt" because it is impossible to live up to every one else's convictions.

Instead, spend time directly listening to the Lord. How? First through reading His Word. That is why this book includes an extensive Bible study section with each chapter – so you can see what the Bible says about these things. Perhaps you even skipped those sections as you read. What does this say about you? Do you really think the words of an author are more important than the Word of God? If you did skip the Bible study sections of each chapter, perhaps you should return to them now and see what God says.

Second, you spend time alone with God – in prayer and listening. How does God speak? Through His Word and directly to our hearts, by the Holy Spirit's inner "quiet small voice." But how can you hear this inner voice if you do not quiet yourself and "tune in?" If you are uncertain exactly where God wants you to grow next, how much time have you spent quietly listening to His quiet inner voice? Take some time alone with God and listen. He will sort out all this light and zero in on one area where He wants you to obey.

So if your light is brighter than your life, spend time in the Bible and in prayerful listening to the Holy Spirit's voice. He will direct your steps. He really will!

6. Quit Trying/Start Trusting

The only way you can become more Christlike is through trusting in Christ's atonement. You and I have no power to change ourselves to become like Christ. Christlikeness is not a result of "trying harder." It comes only through God's miraculous intervention in your life, changing you inside, that you can be conformed to the image of Jesus Christ. So quit trying to change on your own power. And start trusting God to change you through His power.

But there's a hitch. God does not change you

automatically. He's not in the business of manipulating spiritual marionettes. You play a role too. The greatest factor in your changing is your own *will to change.* God changes you as you cooperate with Him. What do you really want? If you decide with God, then He works in your life to change you. If you resist His changing grace you are left in your present state – or perhaps you'll slip back to a former state.

So, the real issue is your will. Concerning that particular conviction . . . that thing you are trying to stop or start, if you say, "I will obey," and you mean it with all your heart. God will perform His part – changing you (or beginning to change you). You can't change yourself. But if you decide to change – God will change you.

7. Don't Resist Him

The reason God brings light to you – urging you to stop something or start another thing – is because He really expects you to obey Him. Be careful to avoid delayed obedience. This kind of foot-dragging will sooner or later turn into disobedience.

Both of my sons have chores. One of the chores is to feed the cat each day. When my son gets home from school, his mother sometimes reminds him "Son, remember to feed the cat." He generally agrees to do it right away. Occasionally he continues playing and says "I'll do it in a minute."

As his mother is getting supper ready, she might again say "Did you feed the cat yet?" His response . . . "I'm on my way now." But there are so many delights scattered about the floor on the way to the cat – games, toys, interesting tools . . . so he gets sidetracked playing. After one or two other reminders, he occasionally comes to the supper table, still having not fed the cat. Dad asks, "Son, have you fed the cat?" He responds, "Not yet, Dad, but I'll get to it right after supper."

169

Now I don't know what your family is like. But after three or four of these kinds of delaying tactics his earthly father will act with warm discipline – that is, warm to certain parts of his anatomy!

There is an invisible line between delay and disobedience. At some point, continual foot-dragging becomes outright disobedience.

Likewise, the Lord has such a line each of us can cross. Our foot-dragging can become outright disobedience at some point. Delayed obedience leads to outright resistance. I am convinced that there are churches full of Christians who have crossed this line in their Christian walk. God has been gentle and tender in His conviction. He has prodded, urged, inspired, persuaded and convicted. But these Christians have gotten in the delaying habit. They now find themselves in a tug-of-war with God, resisting His leadings. They are what the Bible calls, "carnal Christians."

Have you come to the point of resisting God's convicting work, until He cannot get you to respond freely with a "Change me" prayer? If so, can outright rebellion be far away? If you are stubbornly refusing to obey Him, won't this lead to a spirit of rebellion? Won't you eventually mentally shake your fist in God's face shouting under your breath "I *won't* change!" Won't this spirit of rebellion eventually lead to your ruin?

So if your light is brighter than your life, and it is because you are dragging your feet, or even because you have been resisting God's prodding, beware! Your resistance could lead to eventual rebellion and your demise. Take heed! Repent of your heavy-handed stubbornness and submit yourself to God's gentle hand.

After all, He isn't planning to make your life miserable! God sends light your way so you will head in a new direction (or stop heading another direction). By obedience you will have the happiest, most fulfilling life. God doesn't want to bludgeon you into a painful path of following Him. Rather, He is a loving Father who wants to bring to your life great meaning and fulfillment.

Have you become like Jeremiah's hardened jar (Jer. 18-19)? Do you find yourself on the opposite end of the rope from Jesus Christ? If so, then go on over to His side. Join Him in this epic adventure of walking in the light. Allow His hands to reshape you. Allow His grace to soften your hardened spirit of resistance. Submit to Him. Say "Have Thy own way, Lord." Let Him be the potter – you become the malleable clay. Let Him melt you . . . mold you . . . after His will. He will make something beautiful out of your life . . . if you'll let Him.

8. Be Filled With the Spirit.

It would be a mistake to end this book without direct reference to the *greatest secret of holy living* – becoming filled with the Holy Spirit. I call it a secret because so few Christians seem to be aware of the Holy Spirit's filling and even fewer seem to take advantage of it. It's really not a secret at all; it is plain to see throughout Scripture.

Sure, there is sometimes a confusing chorus insisting variously on what this second crisis is all about. And while there are admitted differences in how various church groups interpret this experience, the Bible simply cuts through the whole discussion with the call, "be filled with the Spirit" (Eph. 5:18).

What does the filling of the Spirit have to do with a Christian's spiritual growth? In this spiritual event God performs two mighty transactions in the believer's life – and both have to do with walking in obedience. These two transactions: empowering and cleansing.

Power.

All Christians have the Holy Spirit – you received this Spirit of God when you became a Christian. But all Christians are not *filled* with the Spirit. When the Spirit fills a believer he or she receives *power* (Acts 1:8). What is the power for? It is to activate the believer . . . to energize the Christian to do God's work in this present world. The filling with the Spirit may come with certain emotions and outward experiences, but its purpose is not to tickle our emotions and delight our sensations. The Spirit's filling comes with power to be directed outward toward others.

Cleansing.
There is another side to the Holy Spirit's filling. The Spirit not only empowers, but cleanses too. When a believer is filled with the Spirit, his or her rebellious spirit can be corrected. That resistant attitude towards God's work in our lives can be straightened out. The Holy Spirit will both fill you with power for service and free you from the bondage of a rebellious spirit . . . if you'll let Him.

How? How can you be filled with the Spirit? Three simple steps: (1) Abandon all known sin – decide to walk away from any thought, word or deed of disobedience. (2) Surrender your all to Christ – in one transaction consecrate your total being, past, present, and future, to Jesus Christ alone. (3) Receive the filling of the Holy Spirit by faith – just like you were saved by faith, so now receive the fullness of the Spirit by faith.

That's it. Simple steps to discover this great secret of spiritual growth. If you follow these steps today, you could be filled with the Spirit yet today. Not that they are some sort of ritual or anything like that. You must really mean what you are doing – truly abandoning sin, really surrendering your all to Jesus, and actually receiving this second work of God's grace by faith.

If you take these steps, be prepared for a mighty change in your life. Some have imagined that a person filled with the Spirit is a "finished product" and no more growth would ever occur. Wrong! The Spirit-filled believer will grow *more* in his or her walk of holiness. Why? Because the single greatest barrier to a carnal Christian's growth is a rebellious will . . . a resistant spirit. In the Holy Spirit's cleansing work, this crooked spirit is somehow brought into alignment. God creates a new heart in the believer . . . and grants him or her a "willing spirit" (Ps. 51:10-12).

Now what about you, my friend?

Perhaps you are turned off by this talk of holiness, cleansing, power, and becoming Spirit-filled. Maybe some person claiming to be Spirit-filled tried to coerce you into having an experience like theirs, or to prove they are filled by showing off one particular gift or behavior. Perhaps you have even said to yourself "I'll *never* try that."

This book would not attempt to persuade you to receive something from God you cannot believe and do not desire. But if you do admit to a spirit of resistance to God's work in your life, please give God a fair chance to convince you. Perhaps He is able to do much more than you could even ask Him to do . . . maybe more than you could imagine? Could He do all this through the Holy Spirit's power which is already at work within you (Eph. 3:20)?

Why not look into His Word? Listen to His quiet inner voice. See if *He* is calling you to this work of His grace. Perhaps there is power you don't have? Is there cleansing you haven't received? If so, see what *He* calls you to. The God who calls you is faithful . . . He will do it (1 Thess. 5:23-24). He really will!

Bible Study

1. Matthew 13:1-23. This is a parable Jesus himself explained. If you considered the "seed" in this parable as truth we need to obey (what we have called "light") . . . how would you apply each of the following elements:

— Pathway hearer:

— Rocky places hearer:

— Thorny ground hearer:

— Thirty times producer:

— Sixty times producer:

— Hundred times producer:

— Can you list conviction or changes you have had in the past which fit-into one or another of the above areas?

2. *Galatians 3:3.* Rewrite this verse in your own words using the words "try" and "trust."

3. *Acts 7:51.*

- These are some of Stephen's last words. It was a speech to the Sanhedrin, the Jewish ruling body, given immediately before he was stoned to death. In what ways did these leaders, along with their fathers, "resist the Holy Spirit?"

- What was the result of their resistance?

4. Acts 1:8. In the last words of Jesus, what does He promise His followers will receive after the Holy Spirit comes upon them?

5. Acts 2–8. For each of the scripture quotes below, list what happened and its result.

— *Acts 2:1-4; 41.*

— *Acts 4:31-35.*

— *Acts 5:12-14.*

— *Acts 5:28.*

— *Acts 5:42.*

— *Acts 6:7.*

— *Acts 8:4.*

— *Key Question:* What does any of this have to do with being filled with the Spirit?

6. *Ephesians 5:18.* What are we called to experience here?

7. *Romans 15:16.* Why did Paul think God called him to minister to the Gentiles? How might they become an acceptable offering to God?

8. *Personal Reflection.* What could and should I do in response to the truths I have discovered in this chapter?

— An action to take:

— A promise to make: